NEW YORK TEST PREP

Common Core

English Language Arts

Practice Workbook

Grade 3

ISBN 978-1726427142

TEST MASTER PRESS

www.testmasterpress.com

CONTENTS

INTRODUCTION
For Parents, Teachers, and Tutors

Preparing for the New York State English Language Arts Test

This workbook will prepare students for the New York State English Language Arts Test. On these tests, students read literary and informational passages and answer multiple-choice, short-response, and extended-response questions. This workbook will give students practice answering all these types of questions. It also focuses on developing the key skills that are the basis of the more rigorous tests, including close reading, using evidence from texts, and analyzing and evaluating texts.

Types of Questions on the New York State English Language Arts Test

The test contains multiple-choice (MC), short-response (SR), and extended-response (ER) questions.

- Multiple-choice - students select the one correct answer from four possible options.
- Short-response - students provide a written answer of a few sentences or complete a diagram.
- Extended-response - students provide a written answer of from 1 to 2 pages.

This workbook contains all these types of questions. By completing the practice sets, students will become familiar with all the question types they will encounter on the real test.

Key Features of the New York State Tests

The New York State tests are more rigorous than previous tests and emphasize certain skills. This workbook is designed to focus on the following key features of the tests to ensure that students are fully prepared for the more rigorous tests.

- The tests have a greater emphasis on writing skills. Students will have to provide more written answers, as well as write complete essays.
- The tests focus on close reading and using evidence from the texts. Questions will require students to read texts closely and to use specific evidence from the text.
- The tests involve more analysis and evaluation. Instead of only showing they comprehend texts, students will be asked questions that require them to analyze a text closely, evaluate a text, relate to a text, or form and support an opinion about a text.

About the Next Generation Learning Standards

In 2017, the state of New York introduced the Next Generation Learning Standards. These are revised standards that replace the previous Common Core Learning Standards, though remain very close in content. State testing will continue to assess the Common Core Learning Standards until 2020, but the new standards will be gradually implemented over this time. This workbook has aligned all questions to the new Next Generation Learning Standards. However, the questions still also cover the Common Core standards that are assessed on the state tests.

Common Core ELA

Practice Set 1

Literary Text with MC and SR Questions

Instructions

This set has one passage for you to read. The passage is followed by questions.

Read each question carefully. For each multiple-choice question, fill in the circle for the correct answer. For other types of questions, follow the instructions given. Some of the questions require a written answer. Write your answer on the lines provided.

Sarah and Janet

Sarah and her sister Janet were always competing with each other. Sarah always wanted to outdo Janet. Janet always wanted to outdo Sarah.

They liked most of the same things and this often led to fights. If Janet sang a song, Sarah wanted to sing it louder and better. If Sarah learned a new song on the piano, Janet had to learn it too and she would try to perform it better. They both wanted to be the fastest runner and the best volleyball player. They would even compete over who could finish reading a book the fastest. It drove their mother crazy.

"Why can't you girls just get along?" she would ask them time and time again. "I am so tired of hearing your bickering."

They would just shrug and keep on arguing. One day, their mother had an idea to help them get along. She planned to take them shopping at the local mall. The girls were excited about taking a shopping trip.

"Now you can both pick out something," said their mother as she parked the car outside the mall. "But choose carefully because you can each only have one outfit."

When they arrived at the mall, they entered a clothing shop. Soon enough, the girls began fighting over the clothing.

"I want this dress," Sarah stated.

"No, I want that dress," Janet said.

"I'm having it because it'll look better on me," Sarah said.

"It will not! It will look better on me," Janet said.

"Alright," said their mother quietly. "Since you both like the dress so much, you can both have one. But do you want to each pick a different color?"

"I want the blue one," Sarah quickly stated.

"No, you should get the yellow one. It would look so nice on you," Janet replied.

"You just want me to get the yellow one because you want the blue one," Sarah argued. "But I'm not being fooled. I'm getting the blue one and you can choose whatever one you want."

"Fine. Then I'm getting the blue one too."

Their mother sighed and took the two blue dresses up to the counter. She handed both Sarah and Janet their new dress and they all left the store.

The girls looked at each other. They were both confused. Usually their mother would buy them different clothes. She had never bought them the same thing before. They were happy to get what they wanted, but they returned home unsure as to what was happening.

It all became clear the following day. The girls dressed for school in their own rooms and headed downstairs for breakfast. They were shocked to see that they were both wearing the same outfit. They began to argue about who should go and change their clothes.

"Nobody is going to change their clothes," said their mother. "You both chose these clothes, so you can both wear them. Now you can see what your silly arguments have led to."

The girls giggled as they realized what their mother was saying.

1   What does the word <u>bickering</u> mean in the sentence below?

      "I am so tired of hearing your bickering."

    Ⓐ   Fighting

    Ⓑ   Complaining

    Ⓒ   Singing

    Ⓓ   Competing

2   Which meaning of the word <u>clear</u> is used in the sentence below?

      It all became clear the following day.

    Ⓐ   Able to be seen through

    Ⓑ   Fine or nice

    Ⓒ   Understood or known

    Ⓓ   Sounding pleasant

3   Complete the web with **three** more examples of Sarah and Janet competing with each other.

Playing the piano	
Things that Sarah and Janet Compete Over	

4   What is the mother's main problem in the passage?

Ⓐ   Her daughters have too many things.

Ⓑ   Her daughters need more clothes.

Ⓒ   Her daughters wear the same outfits.

Ⓓ   Her daughters are always fighting.

5   Which sentence spoken by the mother best supports your answer to Question 4?

Ⓐ   *"Why can't you girls just get along?"*

Ⓑ   *"But choose carefully because you can each only have one outfit."*

Ⓒ   *"But do you want to each pick a different color?"*

Ⓓ   *"You both chose these clothes, so you can both wear them."*

6   Read this sentence from the passage.

> **"Why can't you girls just get along?" she would ask them time and time again.**

What does the phrase "time and time again" suggest?

Ⓐ   That the mother has asked the question for the last time

Ⓑ   That the mother asks at the same time each day

Ⓒ   That the mother has asked the question many times

Ⓓ   That the mother asked the question once an hour

7   Where would this passage most likely be found?

    Ⓐ   In a book of poems

    Ⓑ   In a magazine

    Ⓒ   In a science textbook

    Ⓓ   In a book of short stories

8   What most likely happens next in the passage?

    Ⓐ   The girls go shopping again

    Ⓑ   The girls go to school looking the same

    Ⓒ   The girls put on a different matching outfit

    Ⓓ   The girls ask their father for help

9   What happens right after the girls come downstairs for breakfast?

    Ⓐ   They see that they are wearing the same thing.

    Ⓑ   They begin to argue.

    Ⓒ   They start giggling.

    Ⓓ   They get dressed for school.

10   If the passage was given another title, which title would best fit?

    Ⓐ   Being Your Best

    Ⓑ   How to Shop Well

    Ⓒ   Fighting Over Nothing

    Ⓓ   The Magic Dress

11   Explain why you chose the title in Question 10. In your answer, describe how the title you chose tells the theme. Use **two** details from the passage to support your response.

_____

_____

_____

_____

_____

12   Think about how the girls are always competing with each other. Describe **one** way this competing could be good for them.

_____

_____

_____

_____

_____

END OF PRACTICE SET

Common Core ELA

Practice Set 2

Literary Text with MC, SR, and ER Questions

Instructions

This set has one passage for you to read. The passage is followed by questions.

Read each question carefully. For each multiple-choice question, fill in the circle for the correct answer. For other types of questions, follow the instructions given. Some of the questions require a written answer. Write your answer on the lines provided.

The Top of the Tower

1 Toby had a fear of heights. He had carried it with him since he was an infant. As a teenager, his fear had only become worse. He talked to his father about it one day.

2 "I have had enough Dad," he said. "I would love to go rock climbing with my friends. But every time I get too high, I feel sick."

3 His dad paused as he thought about his son's problem.

4 "Well Toby," he said quietly, "I can help you. But you will need to face your fear. Are you ready?"

5 Toby was quiet for a moment.

6 "I am ready!" he replied bravely.

7 Toby's father picked up the keys and walked toward the front door.

8 "We're going into the city!" his father said.

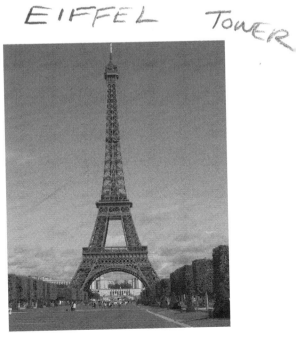

9 Toby knew what was coming. Toby lived in Paris, France. Located in the heart of Paris, was one of the world's tallest landmarks. It was the Eiffel Tower. Toby knew that visitors were allowed to climb to the very top. The view overlooked the entire city. Nothing was said between the pair as they drove into the city.

10 They had arrived at the Eiffel Tower when Toby looked up at it and gasped. His stomach turned over.

11 "I'm not sure if I can do this," he said nervously.

12   Toby's father sensed his son's worries.

13   "Don't worry," he said. "I will be with you every step of the way. This is the day that you beat your fears."

14   Toby stared up at the giant tower. He took a deep breath as they stepped through the entrance. As his father held his hand, they made their way, step by step, towards the top of the building. Once they reached the top, Toby stepped out from the shadows and onto the ledge.

15   "Wow, Dad!" he said excitedly as he looked over Paris. The city looked so beautiful from the tower that his fear began to fade. He kept his hand firmly on the tower's metal railing just in case. It felt strong and steady. He still felt a small knot of fear in his stomach, but he told himself that he was fine. Just like the tower, he felt strong and steady.

16   "I told you there was nothing to worry about," his father said.

1   What does the phrase "heart of" mean in the sentence below?

Located in the heart of Paris, was one of the world's tallest landmarks.

Ⓐ   Streets of

Ⓑ   Edge of

Ⓒ   Center of

Ⓓ   City of

2   Read this sentence from the passage.

Nothing was said between the pair as they drove into the city.

Why was Toby most likely quiet?

Ⓐ   He was fighting with his father.

Ⓑ   He was feeling scared.

Ⓒ   He was excited.

Ⓓ   He was having a nap.

3   Based on the second paragraph, what is the main reason Toby wants to change?

Ⓐ   He does not like being teased.

Ⓑ   He wants to make his father proud.

Ⓒ   He is scared that things will get worse.

Ⓓ   He is tired of missing out on doing things.

4   Describe **two** details from the passage that show that Toby feels nervous about climbing the Eiffel Tower.

1: _he isd frad of hites_

2: _he helled hands with his dad_

5   Read this sentence from the passage.

> **As his father held his hand, they made their way, step by step, towards the top of the building.**

What do the words "step by step" suggest?

Ⓐ   They moved quite slowly.

Ⓑ   They walked a long way.

Ⓒ   They raced each other.

Ⓓ   They made a lot of noise.

6   Who is telling the story?

Ⓐ   Toby

Ⓑ   Toby's father

Ⓒ   A friend of Toby's

Ⓓ   Someone not in the story

7   The main theme of the passage is about –

Ⓐ   taking chances

Ⓑ   overcoming fears

Ⓒ   making friends

Ⓓ   asking for help

8   In the second last paragraph, Toby is described as feeling "strong and steady." The word <u>steady</u> probably means that he feels –

Ⓐ   scared

Ⓑ   sick

Ⓒ   calm

Ⓓ   joyful

9   Complete these sentences. Write **one** of the words below on each line.

shy   calm   afraid   amazed

brave   silly   kind   rude

When Toby looks up at the tower, he feels _afraid_

When Toby climbs the tower, he is being _brave_

10   How do you think Toby feels at the end of the passage? Use **two** details from the passage to support your response.

_____

_____

_____

_____

_____

11   What is Toby's main problem in the passage? How does Toby overcome the problem? Use **two** details from the passage to support your response.

_____

_____

_____

_____

_____

12 The passages describes a character who has a problem. Think about the role the father plays in helping Toby. Write an essay that describes how the father helps Toby solve his problem.

In your response, be sure to
blem that Toby has
father helps Toby solve the problem
the passage to support your answer

END OF PRACTICE SET

Common Core ELA

Practice Set 3

Informational Text with MC and SR Questions

Instructions

This set has one passage for you to read. The passage is followed by questions.

Read each question carefully. For each multiple-choice question, fill in the circle for the correct answer. For other types of questions, follow the instructions given. Some of the questions require a written answer. Write your answer on the lines provided.

Yard Sales

A yard sale is when you sell items in your front yard. People often have yard sales to get rid of unwanted items. It can also be a good way to make some extra money. Here are some tips on how to have a good yard sale.

Finding the Items

1. You need a lot of items to sell. Search your home for all your unwanted items. Make sure everyone in the family joins in. Try to get a large range of items.

2. Clean out the garage or basement. Many people have a store of old stuff somewhere. Offer to clean up this area. As you do, collect everything you think you can sell.

3. Ask other people you know to join in. Many people have junk lying around they want to get rid of. They may be happy to give it to you to sell.

Setting It Up

1. Collect everything you have to sell. It is a good idea to make everything look neat and tidy. If you have clothes, wash them and hang them up. They may not be new clothes, but they'll have to look fresh and clean if you want people to buy them. Clean and dust all the items so they look their best.

2. Set up tables in your front yard to place all the items on. If you are placing items on the ground, put them on a sheet or blanket.

3. People will need to know how much each item is. Put a sticker on each item and write the price on it.

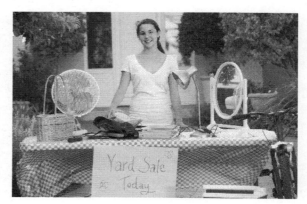

4. Collect some change. People will often pay in notes. Make sure you have plenty of coins to give as change.

Getting a Crowd

1. You want lots of people to come to your yard sale. Here are some things you should do:

- Tell all your friends
- Put notices on notice boards
- Put up flyers
- Put an ad in the local newspaper
- Put a sign at the end of your street

2. Make it easy for people to find the yard sale. Put balloons at the end of your street and in your front yard.

Time to Sell

1. Now it is time to sell your items. Remember that you are selling things you don't really want. Don't try to sell your items for too much. Be open to haggling too. Many people will want a bargain and may not want to pay what you think it's worth. If people suggest a lower price, take it! If people are thinking about buying something, make them a deal.

2. If items are not selling, lower the prices. It is better to sell items for something than to have to pack them all up again.

Popular Yard Sale Items
children's toys
clothes
building materials
furniture
kitchen items
books and movies

1   Read this sentence from the passage.

People often have yard sales to get rid of unwanted items.

What does the word <u>unwanted</u> mean?

Ⓐ   Less wanted

Ⓑ   Used to be wanted

Ⓒ   More wanted

Ⓓ   Not wanted

2   Why should you put balloons in your front yard?

Ⓐ   So people feel good about buying

Ⓑ   So you can sell them

Ⓒ   So people can find your yard sale

Ⓓ   So you can put prices on them

3   If the passage was given another title, which of these would best fit?

Ⓐ   How to Make Money

Ⓑ   How to Hold a Yard Sale

Ⓒ   The Amazing Yard Sale

Ⓓ   Cleaning Up Your House

4   Read this sentence from the passage.

It is a good idea to make everything look neat and tidy.

Which word means the opposite of <u>neat</u>?

Ⓐ   Messy

Ⓑ   Clean

Ⓒ   Dirty

Ⓓ   Nice

5   Which section of the passage describes how to let people know about your yard sale?

Ⓐ   Finding the Items

Ⓑ   Setting It Up

Ⓒ   Getting a Crowd

Ⓓ   Time to Sell

6   According to the passage, which of the following should you do first?

Ⓐ   Set up tables

Ⓑ   Clean all the items

Ⓒ   Put stickers on the items

Ⓓ   Lower the prices

7   How does the information in the table help the reader?

    Ⓐ   It explains how much money can be made.

    Ⓑ   It shows what sort of items to collect.

    Ⓒ   It shows how to price items.

    Ⓓ   It explains why you should have a yard sale.

8   Which phrase from "Time to Sell" best helps you understand the meaning of <u>haggling</u>? Tick the box of the phrase you have selected.

    ☐   "now it is time"

    ☐   "things you don't really want"

    ☐   "many people"

    ☐   "suggest a lower price"

    ☐   "thinking about buying"

9   Describe **two** things the art in the passage helps you understand.

    1: _____

    _____

    2: _____

    _____

10   Draw lines to match each sentence in the first paragraph with its main purpose.

| A yard sale is when you sell items in your front yard. | | to give a second reason for having a yard sale |

| People have yard sales to get rid of unwanted items. | | to tell what a yard sale is |

| It can also be a good way to make some extra money. | | to give the main reason for having a yard sale |

| Here are some tips on how to have a good yard sale. | | to tell what the passage is about |

11   In "Finding the Items," the author suggests that you ask other people to join in. Explain why you think this would be a good idea. Use **two** details from the passage to support your response.

_____

_____

_____

_____

_____

12   Sort the list of things to do below into things that would be best to do in the week before your yard sale and things that would be best to do on the day of your yard sale. Write **three** of the items in each column.

put up flyers   put balloons up   set up the tables

tell your friends   put a sign in your street   run a newspaper ad

The Week Before Your Yard Sale	On the Day of Your Yard Sale

END OF PRACTICE SET

Common Core ELA

Practice Set 4

Informational Text with MC, SR, and ER Questions

Instructions

This set has one passage for you to read. The passage is followed by questions.

Read each question carefully. For each multiple-choice question, fill in the circle for the correct answer. For other types of questions, follow the instructions given. Some of the questions require a written answer. Write your answer on the lines provided.

Summer Lemonade

Lemonade is one of the most popular summer drinks in the United States. It is refreshing and helps you to cool down during the hot summer months. Lemonade is available in most stores and can be purchased as a premade drink. These brands are often made with added sugar and other chemicals. These ingredients often make the drink unhealthy. So we're going to make a healthy homemade lemonade!

To make our own lemonade at home we'll need the right ingredients. You will need 1 cup of sugar, 6 lemons, 1 cup of boiling water, and 4 cups of cold water. You will also need a saucepan and a large pitcher.

Step 1
Start by placing the sugar in a saucepan. Then add the boiling water and heat the mixture gently.

Step 2
Extract the juice from your 6 lemons. You can use a juicer. Or you can squeeze them by hand. Add the lemon juice to the water and sugar mixture.

Step 3
Pour the mixture into a pitcher. Then take your 4 cups of cold water and add these to the pitcher. This will cool the mixture down and make it ready to refrigerate. The amount of cold water that you add will affect the strength of the lemonade. You can add more water if you like it weaker.

Step 4
Refrigerate the mixture for 30 or 40 minutes. Taste your lemonade mixture. If it is too sweet, add a little more lemon juice. If it is too strong, add some more water. If it is too sour, add some more sugar.

Step 5
You are now ready to serve your lemonade. Pour it into a glass with ice and a slice of lemon.

Now that you know how to make lemonade, why not use this new skill to make some money on the weekend? Make a nice big batch of lemonade and start a lemonade stand in your front yard. Here are some tips for setting up a good lemonade stand.

1. Make sure you have a good spot. You're usually not allowed to set up stands in public places like parks, so you'll need to do it in your yard. But it's best if you live in a spot where plenty of people will walk past. If your home is not right, consider asking a friend who lives in a better spot to help you. Then you can set up the stand at your friend's house.

2. Get your stand noticed. You want your stand to be easy to spot. Take the time to paint a colorful banner or to put up signs. You can also add things like streamers and balloons. You could also put signs up at the end of your street. Then people will know that fresh lemonade is just around the corner.

3. Choose the right price. You need to make sure you aren't charging too much for your lemonade. It's also easiest if you don't need to worry about giving change. Set your price to $1, $2, or $3. You should also be willing to do deals. If someone wants to buy more than one, offer them a special deal.

4. You want people to want to drink your lemonade, so make sure you present it nicely. You can add a few lemon wedges to the container to make it look nice and fresh. You can also place lemons around your stand as decorations. You should also cover the table you are using with a nice tablecloth. The nicer your stand looks, the more people will want to buy your product.

5. Add other products. Do you have a friend who makes delicious cupcakes or amazing banana bread? Invite them to join in. You can sell treats to go with your fresh lemonade and make even more money.

1   Read this sentence from the passage.

       Lemonade is available in most stores and can be purchased as a premade drink.

       What does the word <u>purchased</u> mean?

       Ⓐ   Made

       Ⓑ   Found

       Ⓒ   Bought

       Ⓓ   Eaten

2   What would be the best way to improve how the information in paragraph 2 is presented?

       Ⓐ   Add bullet points

       Ⓑ   Add a diagram

       Ⓒ   Add a chart

       Ⓓ   Add a graph

3   What is the main purpose of the passage?

       Ⓐ   To instruct

       Ⓑ   To entertain

       Ⓒ   To inform

       Ⓓ   To persuade

4 In which step is the sugar first needed? Circle the correct step.

Step 1   Step 2   Step 3   Step 4   Step 5

5 As it is used below, which word means the opposite of <u>weaker</u>?

You can add more water if you like it weaker.

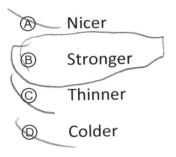

- Ⓐ   Nicer
- Ⓑ   Stronger
- Ⓒ   Thinner
- Ⓓ   Colder

6 Complete the diagram by writing **one** of the sentences below in each box.

Add water.   Add lemon juice.   Add sugar.

Problem with the Lemonade   How to Solve the Problem

Problem with the Lemonade	How to Solve the Problem
It is too sour.	Add sugar
It is too sweet.	Add lemon juice
It is too strong.	add water

7   According to the passage, why is homemade lemonade better than lemonade from a store?

    Ⓐ   It lasts longer.

    Ⓑ   It is cheaper.

    Ⓒ   It is better for you.

    Ⓓ   It is easier to make.

8   What is the main purpose of the first paragraph?

    Ⓐ   To describe how to make lemonade

    Ⓑ   To encourage people to want to make lemonade

    Ⓒ   To tell what lemonade is made from

    Ⓓ   To explain where to get lemonade from

9   Based on the information in the passage, describe **two** ways asking a friend to help with your lemonade stand would help you.

1: _to make people get more snacks_

2: _you can set up the stand at your frends house_

10   Write the name of each item used to make the lemonade in the order they are added.

boiling   cold water   lemons   sugar
water

| Sugar | → | hot water | → | lemons | → | cold water |

11   Do you feel it would be worth it to set up a lemonade stand? Explain why or why not. Use **two** details from the passage to support your response.

yes becanse I have
a plase to put it. also becans
I call make the lemonade
good

12   The passage gives an idea for making money on the weekend. Write an article for your school newspaper suggesting that students set up a lemonade stand on the weekend.

In your response, be sure to
- describe how students can make money
- tell some of the benefits of a lemonade stand
- give some advice for making the event a success
- use details from the passage

_____

_____

_____

_____

_____

_____

_____

_____

_____

_____

_____

_____

END OF PRACTICE SET

Common Core ELA

Practice Set 5

Literary Text with MC, SR, and ER Questions

Instructions

This set has one passage for you to read. The passage is followed by questions.

Read each question carefully. For each multiple-choice question, fill in the circle for the correct answer. For other types of questions, follow the instructions given. Some of the questions require a written answer. Write your answer on the lines provided.

A Special Day

Dear Uncle Yuri,

Today was quite an amazing day for me. It was the day that my father returned home from overseas. He had been away from us for over a year. He was chosen to work on a special research project in London. He and his team were working on a new way to make recycled paper products. It would use less water and energy and be better for the environment. Although we were proud of him, we longed for the day when he would wake up under the same roof as us. We had missed him more than words could ever say. Now the day had finally arrived. He had worked hard and it was time for him to return home.

Mom woke us at 6 a.m. to head to the airport. My father's flight was due in at 9:30. "We don't want to be late!" she kept saying as she woke everyone up. She had no need to remind me! I quickly dressed, washed, and made my way downstairs for breakfast. I could not take my eyes off the clock all morning. Time was going so slowly. When the clock struck 8:45, my mom told us all it was time to go. We all raced to the car and made our way quickly to the airport.

We arrived just after 9 and hurried to the terminal to wait. But 9:30 came and went and our father's flight had still not arrived. Another 10 minutes went by, and I started pacing up and down. I kept asking Mom where he was. She just kept smiling and saying he'd be there soon. I searched the crowds of people, hoping to see his familiar face. I stood as tall as I could to try and see every person coming through the gate.

Then suddenly a gap appeared in the crowd and a tall shadow emerged. There was my father standing before me. He dropped his bags to the floor and swept my sister and I up in his arms. "I've missed you so much," he said through tears of joy. We all cried together. I never want my father to ever let me go.

Today was pretty perfect.

Holly

1   Read this sentence from the letter.

I could not take my eyes off the clock all morning.

This sentence shows that Holly was –

Ⓐ   worried

Ⓑ   excited

Ⓒ   bored

Ⓓ   patient

2   Why does Holly most likely say that she doesn't need to be reminded not to be late?

Ⓐ   She does not care if they are late.

Ⓑ   She knows that the plane will be late.

Ⓒ   She would never want to be late.

Ⓓ   She thinks that they will be late anyway.

3   The second paragraph starts with the sentence "Mom woke us at 6 a.m. to head to the airport." How is the second paragraph mainly organized?

Ⓐ   A problem is described and then a solution is given.

Ⓑ   Events are described in the order they occur.

Ⓒ   Facts are given to support an argument.

Ⓓ   A question is asked and then answered.

4   The reader can tell that Holly's father –

    Ⓐ   missed his family very much

    Ⓑ   wants to go overseas again

    Ⓒ   is surprised to be home

    Ⓓ   thinks his kids have grown up a lot

5   How does Holly most likely feel while waiting at the airport?

    Ⓐ   Surprised

    Ⓑ   Anxious

    Ⓒ   Calm

    Ⓓ   Bored

6   Based on your answer to Question 5, describe **two** details given about Holly that show how she feels while waiting at the airport.

1: _____

_____

2: _____

_____

7   Which sentence from the letter best shows how Holly feels about having her father home?

    Ⓐ   *There was my father standing before me.*

    Ⓑ   *He dropped his bags to the floor and swept my sister and I up in his arms.*

    Ⓒ   *We all cried together.*

    Ⓓ   *I never want my father to ever let me go.*

8   Read this sentence from the letter.

We had missed him more than words could ever say.

Which literary device is used in this sentence?

    Ⓐ   Imagery, using details to create an image or picture

    Ⓑ   Hyperbole, using exaggeration to make a point

    Ⓒ   Simile, comparing two items using the words "like" or "as"

    Ⓓ   Symbolism, using an object to stand for something else

9   Which sentence from the letter best explains why Holly is looking forward to seeing her father so much?

    Ⓐ   *Today was quite an amazing day for me.*

    Ⓑ   *He had been away from us for over a year.*

    Ⓒ   *My father's flight was due in at 9:30.*

    Ⓓ   *Time was going so slowly.*

10   The photograph in the passage mainly helps show that the airport was –

    (A)   clean

    (B)   loud

    (C)   crowded

    (D)   cold

11   Read this sentence from the passage.

> **He dropped his bags to the floor and swept my sister and I up in his arms.**

Explain what the father's actions in this sentence show about how he feels. Use **two** details from the passage to support your response.

_____

_____

_____

_____

_____

_____

12   The passage tells about the first time Holly saw her father again after he was away for a year. How does the author build suspense as the passage reaches its turning point? Use details from the passage to support your response.

In your response, be sure to
- identify the turning point of the passage
- explain how the author builds suspense
- use details from the passage to support your answer

_____

_____

_____

_____

_____

_____

_____

_____

_____

_____

_____

END OF PRACTICE SET

Common Core ELA

Practice Set 6

Literary Text with MC and SR Questions

Instructions

This set has one passage for you to read. The passage is followed by questions.

Read each question carefully. For each multiple-choice question, fill in the circle for the correct answer. For other types of questions, follow the instructions given. Some of the questions require a written answer. Write your answer on the lines provided.

The Wiggly Worm

3/19/20

The worm is one of nature's
most wonderful of creatures,
as it slinks beneath the soil,
with all its special features.

The worm is an explorer,
of both soft and well-worn land,
on a journey through the landscape,
unearthing stones, loose earth, and sand.

Though they barely see above the grass,
they see all beneath the ground,
hiding amongst the flower beds,
as they wiggle round and round.

Their bodies are long and slender
and as light as summer's breeze,
gilding shapes beneath the surface,
with slow and steady ease.

They're the envy of the rhino,
the hippopotamus, and ape,
and all the other animals that lack
one single beautiful shape.

So when you see the wiggly worm,
smile at his simple form,
and ponder his adventures,
in the earth all wet and warm.

1   Read this line from the poem.

           they see all beneath the ground,

       Which word means the opposite of <u>beneath</u>?

       Ⓐ   Below

       Ⓑ   Above

       Ⓒ   Far

       Ⓓ   Along

2   Write the **two** words that best complete the sentence on the lines.

           scary   amazing   ugly   boring

           dirty   beautiful   sad   lonely

       The poet would most likely describe worms as _____dirty_____ and
       _____ugly_____ .

3   What is the rhyme pattern of each stanza of the poem?

       Ⓐ   The second and fourth lines rhyme.

       Ⓑ   There are two pairs of rhyming lines.

       Ⓒ   The first and last lines rhyme.

       Ⓓ   None of the lines rhyme.

4   Which line from the poem contains a simile?

   Ⓐ   *as it slinks beneath the soil,*

   Ⓑ   *hiding amongst the flower beds,*

   Ⓒ   *and as light as summer's breeze,*

   Ⓓ   *So when you see the wiggly worm,*

5   Which words from the poem describe what a worm looks like?

   Ⓐ   *soft and well-worn*

   Ⓑ   *long and slender*

   Ⓒ   *slow and steady*

   Ⓓ   *wet and warm*

6   Select **all** the lines below that contain alliteration.

   ☑   *most wonderful of creatures,*

   ☐   *with all its special features.*

   ☑   *The worm is an explorer,*

   ☑   *they see all beneath the ground,*

   ☐   *with slow and steady ease.*

   ☐   *and ponder his adventures,*

   ☐   *in the earth all wet and warm.*

7   The poet describes worms as explorers. What makes a worm like an explorer? In your answer, explain what worms explore. Use **two** details from the passage to support your response.

They look
around

8   The poet tries to get readers to feel like worms are interesting and special. Do you feel that the poet is successful? Use **two** details from the passage to support your response.

The worm is most
wonderful of creatures

9   According to the poem, why is the worm the envy of the rhino, hippopotamus, and ape? Explain what the worm has that these animals do not. Use **two** details from the passage to support your response.

the worm has

a shape

10   What does the poet mainly want readers to learn from the poem?

Ⓐ   Where worms can be found

Ⓑ   Why worms are useful

Ⓒ   How interesting worms are

Ⓓ   How worms are able to move

END OF PRACTICE SET

Common Core ELA

Practice Set 7

Literary Text with MC, SR, and ER Questions

Instructions

This set has one passage for you to read. The passage is followed by questions.

Read each question carefully. For each multiple-choice question, fill in the circle for the correct answer. For other types of questions, follow the instructions given. Some of the questions require a written answer. Write your answer on the lines provided.

The Bumble Bee

Yellow and black with a set of tiny wings,
I busily buzz around the land,
And boast a mighty sting!

I do not care for fame or money,
I do not wish to harm,
I just live for making honey!

This beekeeper holds up honeycomb that has been made in the hive. The honey is extracted, or taken out, from the honeycomb. Bees can sting, so this beekeeper wears a special bee suit to keep him safe. Bees usually only sting when they are afraid of something. The best way to be safe from bees is simply to leave them alone!

1   According to the poem, what does the bee enjoy most?

    Ⓐ   Being famous

    Ⓑ   Being rich

    Ⓒ   Making honey

    Ⓓ   Stinging people

2   Read this line from the poem.

I busily buzz around the land,

Which literary device is used in this line?

    Ⓐ   Alliteration

    Ⓑ   Simile

    Ⓒ   Metaphor

    Ⓓ   Imagery

3   What is the rhyme pattern of each stanza of the poem?

    Ⓐ   Every line rhymes.

    Ⓑ   The first and second lines rhyme.

    Ⓒ   The first and last lines rhyme.

    Ⓓ   None of the lines rhyme.

4   Onomatopoeia is when a word sounds like what it describes. Which word from the poem is an example of onomatopoeia?

Ⓐ   *black*

Ⓑ   *wings*

Ⓒ   *buzz*

Ⓓ   *sting*

5   In the line below, what does the word <u>mighty</u> mean?

And boast a mighty sting!

Ⓐ   Scary

Ⓑ   Strange

Ⓒ   Naughty

Ⓓ   Great

6   Which sentence from the caption best supports the idea that bees do not wish to harm?

Ⓐ   *This beekeeper holds up honeycomb that has been made in the hive.*

Ⓑ   *The honey is extracted, or taken out, from the honeycomb.*

Ⓒ   *Bees can sting, so this beekeeper wears a special bee suit to keep him safe.*

Ⓓ   *Bees usually only sting when they are afraid of something.*

7   What does the photograph help readers understand? Use **two** details from the passage to support your response.

_____

_____

_____

_____

_____

8   Complete the diagram below by listing **three** facts the author gives about bees.

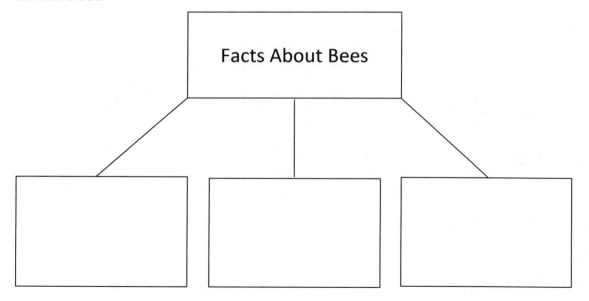

9   While bees can be dangerous, do you think most poeple need to fear bees? Use **two** details from the passage to support your response.

_____

_____

_____

_____

_____

10 Think about the point of view of the poem. Who is the speaker in the poem? How does this point of view affect the poem? In your answer, explain whether or not it helps readers take the poem seriously. Use details from the poem to support your answer.

In your response, be sure to
- identify the point of view of the poem
- describe how the point of view affects readers of the poem
- explain whether the point of view helps readers take the poem seriously
- use details from the poem to support your answer

_____

_____

_____

_____

_____

_____

_____

_____

_____

_____

_____

END OF PRACTICE SET

Common Core ELA

Practice Set 8

Informational Text with MC and SR Questions

Instructions

This set has one passage for you to read. The passage is followed by questions.

Read each question carefully. For each multiple-choice question, fill in the circle for the correct answer. For other types of questions, follow the instructions given. Some of the questions require a written answer. Write your answer on the lines provided.

A Letter to My Favorite Author

July 1, 2018

Dear Simeon,

I am writing to tell you what a huge fan I am of your work. I have enjoyed your books since I was eight years old. I read a story in the newspaper that said you were ill. It made me feel sad. I wanted to write just to tell you how much I like your work. And that I hope you feel better soon too!

My love for your work began with your first book. *The Singing Swordfish* was so well-written. The pictures also helped to bring your words to life. I laughed so hard I cried the first time I read the book! From then on, I was hooked on your every word. I cannot imagine a better children's author existing anywhere else in the world. If there is one, I would certainly like to know about them too! If I had to choose which of your books was my favorite, it would be *The Shining Light*. That story was such an adventure from start to finish. Your book *Rainy Day* is also a favorite. It made me think a lot about how I treat others. And of course, I love *Just Lazing Around* as well. It always makes me laugh.

I really hope that you feel better soon. You have given so much joy to so many people. Take care and thank you for all of the memories and moments of joy that you have given me. My wish is that you get better soon and keep creating new books for your loyal readers to fall in love with. I can't wait to see what wonderful new adventures you have in store for your readers!

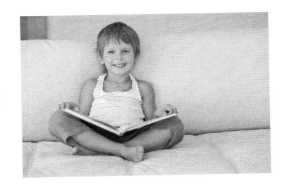

Yours sincerely,

Kyle Harper

1   Read this sentence from the letter.

From then on, I was hooked on your every word.

What does the phrase "hooked on" mean?

Ⓐ   Very keen on

Ⓑ   Confused by

Ⓒ   Bent

Ⓓ   Owned

2   Read this sentence from the letter.

I cannot imagine a better children's author existing anywhere else in the world.

Which word means about the same as <u>existing</u>?

Ⓐ   Living

Ⓑ   Writing

Ⓒ   Working

Ⓓ   Thinking

3   According to the letter, why does Kyle decide to write to Simeon?

      Ⓐ   He is asked to by his mother.

      Ⓑ   He wants to be sent a free book.

      Ⓒ   He wants her to write another book.

      Ⓓ   He reads that she is ill.

4   Based on your answer to Question 3, choose **two** sentences from the first paragraph that support your answer. Circle the **two** sentences below. Then explain why you chose those sentences.

> I am writing to tell you what a huge fan I am of your work. I have enjoyed your books since I was eight years old. I read a story in the newspaper that said you were ill. It made me feel sad. I wanted to write just to tell you how much I like your work. And that I hope you feel better soon too!

_____

_____

_____

_____

_____

5   Complete the chart by writing **one** book from the list below in each space.

The Singing Swordfish   *The Shining Light*

Rainy Day   *Just Lazing Around*

Favorite Book:	
First Book Read:	

6   The reader can tell that Kyle –

Ⓐ   no longer reads Simeon's books

Ⓑ   wants to be a writer someday

Ⓒ   has read many of Simeon's books

Ⓓ   started reading because he was ill

7   What is the first paragraph mainly about?

Ⓐ   Why Kyle is writing to Simeon

Ⓑ   When Kyle started reading Simeon's books

Ⓒ   Which book of Simeon's is Kyle's favorite

Ⓓ   How Kyle reads the newspaper

8   Which part of the letter tells who wrote the letter?

     Ⓐ   Date

     Ⓑ   Greeting

     Ⓒ   Closing

     Ⓓ   Body

9   Describe **two** reasons that Kyle liked the book *The Singing Swordfish*.

     1: _____

     2: _____

10   Do you think Simeon would feel good after reading the letter? Use **two** details from the passage to support your response.

_____

_____

_____

_____

_____

END OF PRACTICE SET

Common Core ELA

Practice Set 9

Informational Text with MC, SR, and ER Questions

Instructions

This set has one passage for you to read. The passage is followed by questions.

Read each question carefully. For each multiple-choice question, fill in the circle for the correct answer. For other types of questions, follow the instructions given. Some of the questions require a written answer. Write your answer on the lines provided.

No Time to Talk

May 23, 2018

Dear Principal Becker,

I understand that school is meant for learning. It is important to have good reading skills and to be able to solve math problems. But I think school is also important for another reason. It helps people learn to get along with others.

It may seem like lunchtime is not important. After all, I spend most lunchtimes just chatting to my friends. But this activity is more important than it looks.

I am learning how to get along with others. I am learning how to solve problems. I am finding out new things from people, and realizing my mistakes. I am learning how to stand up for myself. I am learning how to say sorry. These are all important skills to learn.

My problem is that the time for lunch and our other breaks keep getting shorter. I know this is happening so we can spend more time in class learning. But please do not forget that we are also learning in our lunchtimes. We are learning people skills. It is important that we have enough time to spend with our friends.

I ask that you consider making our lunch break longer. A little more time spent with friends each day would benefit everybody.

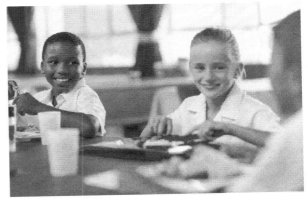

Best,

Simone Anderson

1   Read this sentence from the letter.

My problem is that the time for lunch and our other breaks keep getting shorter.

What does the word <u>shorter</u> mean?

Ⓐ   Less short

Ⓑ   The most short

Ⓒ   More short

Ⓓ   The least short

2   What does the word <u>benefit</u> mean in the sentence below?

A little more time spent with friends each day would benefit everybody.

Ⓐ   Change

Ⓑ   Help

Ⓒ   Interest

Ⓓ   Harm

3   According to the letter, what does Simone learn at lunchtime?

Ⓐ   Math skills

Ⓑ   Reading skills

Ⓒ   People skills

Ⓓ   Drawing skills

4   Why did Simone write the letter?

  Ⓐ   To persuade the principal to do something

  Ⓑ   To entertain the principal

  Ⓒ   To show the principal her writing skills

  Ⓓ   To teach the principal how to do something

5   Which sentence best shows the main idea of the letter?

  Ⓐ   *I understand that school is meant for learning.*

  Ⓑ   *It may seem like lunchtime is not important.*

  Ⓒ   *After all, I spend most lunchtimes just chatting to my friends.*

  Ⓓ   *It is important that we have enough time to spend with our friends.*

6   What is the paragraph below mostly about?

> **I am learning how to get along with others. I am learning how to solve problems. I am finding out new things from people, and realizing my mistakes. I am learning how to stand up for myself. I am learning how to say sorry. These are all important skills to learn.**

  Ⓐ   What Simone learns at lunchtime

  Ⓑ   How long lunchtime lasts for

  Ⓒ   What skills students should be taught

  Ⓓ   What problems Simone has each day

7   Look at the web below.

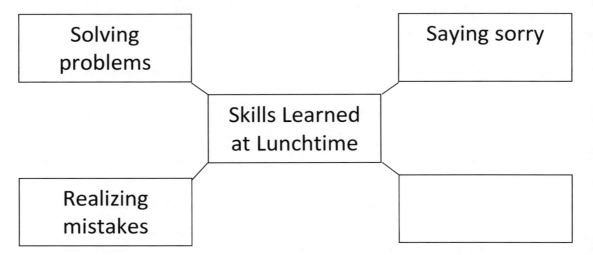

Which of these best completes the web? Write your answer in the web.

Managing time	Reading well

Solving math problems	Standing up for yourself

8   Which statement is most likely true about Simone?

   Ⓐ   She writes a lot of letters to the principal.

   Ⓑ   She spends a lot of time in class talking.

   Ⓒ   She enjoys spending time with her friends.

   Ⓓ   She wishes that her friends were nicer.

9   What are the main benefits of increasing the length of the lunch break? Use **two** details from the passage to support your response.

_____

_____

_____

_____

_____

_____

_____

_____

_____

_____

_____

_____

_____

_____

10   Think about why Simone wrote the letter and who Simone is writing to. Write an essay that describes the purpose, audience, and tone of the letter. Use details from the passage to support your response.

In your response, be sure to
- describe the purpose of the letter
- describe who Simone is writing to
- describe the tone of the letter
- tell how the tone matches the purpose and the audience
- use details from the letter to support your answer

_____

_____

_____

_____

_____

_____

_____

_____

_____

_____

_____

_____

END OF PRACTICE SET

Common Core ELA

Practice Set 10

Literary Text with MC, SR, and ER Questions

Instructions

This set has one passage for you to read. The passage is followed by questions.

Read each question carefully. For each multiple-choice question, fill in the circle for the correct answer. For other types of questions, follow the instructions given. Some of the questions require a written answer. Write your answer on the lines provided.

The Troublemaker

 Kevin had always been known for playing tricks. As he got older, his tricks got worse. Over time, everyone began to know Kevin as a troublemaker. Kevin enjoyed all of the attention. He almost felt famous for his tricks.

One day, he was at his friend Jason's house playing hide and seek. Kevin told Jason to hide from the others in his basement. Jason opened the door and started down the steps. Kevin quickly locked the basement door behind him. Kevin put the key into his pocket and skipped away.

Jason called out to his friends. He couldn't hear a reply, so he called out a little louder. He rattled the doorknob hoping it would open. Then he began banging on the door. Jason's friends heard the sound and raced to the door. They called out to let Jason know they would get him out soon. Jason's friend Max pushed on the door as hard as he could. But the door would not budge.

Eventually, Jason's mother heard the noise and came downstairs. She unlocked the door with a spare key and hugged her son as he ran out.

"Who did this?" she asked firmly.

Kevin smiled and put his hand in the air. Jason's mother sighed.

"You seem very proud, Kevin," she said. "But what you don't realize is that being well-known for something isn't always a good thing. Maybe once you were thought of as funny, but now you're just becoming nasty."

Kevin's shoulders slumped.

"I guess so," he whispered. "I just thought it would be funny. I didn't mean to hurt anybody. But I guess nobody is laughing, are they?"

Kevin decided he would have to be more careful about the jokes he chose to play on his friends.

1   Read these sentences from the passage.

Jason's friend Max pushed on the door as hard as he could. But the door would not budge.

What does the word <u>budge</u> mean in the sentence?

Ⓐ   Break

Ⓑ   Bend

Ⓒ   Move

Ⓓ   Listen

2   Circle the **two** words from the passage that have about the same meaning.

friends   famous   tricks

nasty   proud   well-known

funny   rattled   laughing

3   Who is the main character in the passage?

Ⓐ   Kevin

Ⓑ   Jason's mother

Ⓒ   Jason

Ⓓ   Max

4   Read this sentence from the passage.

Kevin put the key into his pocket and skipped away.

What does the word <u>skipped</u> suggest about Kevin?

Ⓐ   He moved slowly.

Ⓑ   He was happy.

Ⓒ   He moved quietly.

Ⓓ   He was angry.

5   Read the list of the mother's actions in the story. Order the actions from first to last by writing the numbers 1, 2, 3, and 4 on the lines.

____   She asks who locked Jason in the basement.

____   She lets Jason out of the basement.

____   She explains to Kevin why he should not play tricks.

____   She hears a noise coming from the basement.

6   Which word best describes the trick that Kevin plays on Jason?

Ⓐ   Funny

Ⓑ   Mean

Ⓒ   Strange

Ⓓ   Silly

7   What is the second paragraph mostly about?

Ⓐ   Why Kevin plays tricks

Ⓑ   How children should not play in basements

Ⓒ   A trick that Kevin plays on a friend

Ⓓ   How a boy learns why he shouldn't play tricks

8   Which word describes how Jason feels while he is locked in the basement?

Ⓐ   Calm

Ⓑ   Bored

Ⓒ   Angry

Ⓓ   Frightened

9   Choose the **two** sentences from the third paragraph that best support your answer to Question 8. Tick **two** boxes below to show your choices.

☐   Jason called out to his friends.

☐   He couldn't hear a reply, so he called out a little louder.

☐   He rattled the doorknob hoping it would open.

☐   Then he began banging on the door.

☐   Jason's friends heard the sound and raced to the door.

☐   They called out to let Jason know they would get him out soon.

☐   Jason's friend Max pushed on the door as hard as he could.

☐   But the door would not budge.

10   What lesson do you think Kevin learns? Use **two** details from the passage to support your response.

_____

_____

_____

_____

_____

11   Do you think Kevin will keep playing jokes in the future? Explain why or why not. Use **two** details from the passage to support your response.

_____

_____

_____

_____

_____

12   In the story, Kevin plays a trick on Jason. Think about how Jason would feel during the events. Write an essay that describes how Jason probably feels during the main events of the story. Use details from the story to support your answer.

In your response, be sure to
- describe how Jason probably feels while locked in the basement
- describe how Jason probably feels after getting out of the basement
- give your opinion on how Jason probably feels about Kevin
- explain why you think Jason would feel that way
- use details from the story to support your answer

_____

_____

_____

_____

_____

_____

_____

_____

_____

_____

_____

END OF PRACTICE SET

Common Core ELA

Practice Set 11

Informational Text with MC, SR, and ER Questions

Instructions

This set has one passage for you to read. The passage is followed by questions.

Read each question carefully. For each multiple-choice question, fill in the circle for the correct answer. For other types of questions, follow the instructions given. Some of the questions require a written answer. Write your answer on the lines provided.

Roger Federer

Roger Federer is a famous tennis player. He was born in Switzerland in 1981. Some people believe that he is the best tennis player ever. He became the world number one in 2005. He kept this rank for 237 weeks in a row. That is a record! He won 16 Grand Slam titles. That is also a record!

© Derek Holtham

Roger plays well on clay, grass, and hard courts. However, he plays best on grass courts.

Wimbledon is a tennis contest held in Great Britain. Roger has won it six times. In 2008, he tried to win it for the sixth time in a row. He made the final. He was defeated by Spanish player Rafael Nadal. It was a close match. It was tough on both players. It was also great to watch. Some people say that it was the best tennis match ever played. This match also started a long row between the two players.

In 2009, Nadal was having knee problems. He was not well enough to compete in Wimbledon. Federer won that year. In 2010, Nadal beat Roger in the Wimbledon final. The two have competed in eight Grand Slam finals together. Nadal has won six of these.

In 2010, Roger lost his number one ranking. Nadal became world number one. At the start of 2011, Roger was ranked third in the world. In 2017, Nadal was world number 1. Federer beat him in the final of the Shanghai Masters, and then went on to win the Australian Open. He became world number 1 again in February, 2018.

While Federer is known for being best on grass courts, Nadal is known for being best on clay courts. Nadal has even been nicknamed "The King of Clay." However, this doesn't mean he isn't great on other types of surfaces as well. He has won Grand Slam titles on hard court, grass, and clay.

1   Read this sentence from the passage.

This match also started a long row between the two players.

Which word means about the same as <u>row</u>?

Ⓐ   Game

Ⓑ   Chat

Ⓒ   Fight

Ⓓ   Problem

2   In paragraph 3, what does the word <u>defeated</u> mean?

Ⓐ   Beaten

Ⓑ   Watched

Ⓒ   Surprised

Ⓓ   Hurt

3   Where was Roger Federer born?

Ⓐ   Great Britain

Ⓑ   Switzerland

Ⓒ   Spain

Ⓓ   United States

4   What is the first paragraph mainly about?

    Ⓐ   Roger Federer's success

    Ⓑ   Roger Federer's family

    Ⓒ   Roger Federer's problems

    Ⓓ   Roger Federer's childhood

5   Which sentence below is best supported by information in the passage?

    Ⓐ   Nadal dislikes playing Roger Federer.

    Ⓑ   Nadal plays better on clay than Roger Federer.

    Ⓒ   Nadal looked up to Roger Federer when he was young.

    Ⓓ   Nadal is a more exciting player than Roger Federer.

6   Which detail best supports your answer to Question 5?

    Ⓐ   Federer and Nadal played in a match that some people say is the best match ever played.

    Ⓑ   Nadal defeated Federer in 6 out of 8 Grand Slam finals.

    Ⓒ   Nadal has even been nicknamed "The King of Clay."

    Ⓓ   Federer remained as world number one for 237 weeks.

7   Circle the details listed below that are facts. Then add **two** more facts from the passage to the list.

Roger Federer is the best tennis player ever.

Roger Federer was born in 1981.

Roger Federer was number one for 237 weeks in a row.

Roger Federer is a great player to watch.

_____

_____

8   Why didn't Nadal compete in Wimbledon in 2009?

Ⓐ   He was too young.

Ⓑ   He had knee problems.

Ⓒ   He wasn't good enough.

Ⓓ   He had won too many times.

9   How did Roger most likely feel when he lost the 2008 Wimbledon final?

Ⓐ   Calm

Ⓑ   Upset

Ⓒ   Proud

Ⓓ   Scared

10   Read this sentence from the passage.

It was a close match.

In which sentence does the word <u>close</u> mean the same as in the sentence above?

Ⓐ   Kerry tried to <u>close</u> the door quietly.

Ⓑ   They had to <u>close</u> off the street for the parade.

Ⓒ   Joanne and Kendra are <u>close</u> friends.

Ⓓ   James raced past Jonah and won the <u>close</u> race.

11   The author describes a 2008 Wimbledon final between Rafael Nadal and Roger Federer. Describe **two** reasons this match was important. Use information from the passage to support your answer.

_____

_____

_____

_____

_____

_____

12   How does the author show that Roger Federer is a successful tennis
      player? Use at least **three** details from the passage in your answer.

      In your response, be sure to
      •   explain how the author shows that Roger Federer is successful
      •   use at least **three** details from the passage to support your answer

_____

_____

_____

_____

_____

_____

_____

_____

_____

_____

_____

_____

END OF PRACTICE SET

Common Core ELA

Practice Set 12

Literary Text with MC, SR, and ER Questions

Instructions

This set has one passage for you to read. The passage is followed by questions.

Read each question carefully. For each multiple-choice question, fill in the circle for the correct answer. For other types of questions, follow the instructions given. Some of the questions require a written answer. Write your answer on the lines provided.

A Bold Decision

Steven loved playing for his basketball team. He had been playing basketball for as long as he could remember. Last year, they had won the state finals. This year, they were finding things much harder. There were only three games left in the season. Steven's team needed to win them all if they were going to the state playoffs. It was near the end of the game. They were behind by six points. Steven had just saved a basket with a great block. But he had hurt his knee as he landed.

"Are you okay to play?" asked his coach.

Steven frowned at the pain in his knee.

"I'll be fine," he said.

Steven knew the risks of his decision. He could risk hurting his knee even more. Or he could choose not to play. He knew that not playing might cause his team to lose. As he rested before the final quarter, he decided to play through the pain. He was going to win this game for the team he loved.

As the quarter started, he caught the ball after the other team made a mistake. He bounced the ball down the court and threw the ball into the hoop. Steven smiled towards his coach on the sidelines. They were only four points behind now.

Steven kept playing well during the final quarter. He even scored a three point shot from the center of the court. With just two minutes left on the clock, Steven's team was only one point behind. Steven was passed the ball by his teammate. He ignored the pain in his knee and sprinted forward. He headed towards the end of the court. His feet left the ground. He sent his shot into the basket and earned his side two points. The final whistle blew seconds after. Steven's bold decision had won his team the game.

1   In the sentence below, which word could best be used in place of <u>center</u>?

He even scored a three point shot from the center of the court.

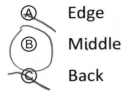

Ⓐ   Edge

Ⓑ   Middle

Ⓒ   Back

Ⓓ   Front

2   Circle the **two** words from the passage that have about the same meaning.

finals   games   rested

decision   threw   choice

3   Which pair of sentences from the first paragraph best tell why the game is important to Steven? Tick **one** box below to show your choice.

☐   Steven loved playing for his basketball team. He had been playing basketball for as long as he could remember.

☒   Last year, they had won the state finals. This year, they were finding things much harder.

☐   There were only three games left in the season. Steven's team needed to win them all if they were going to the state playoffs.

☐   It was near the end of the game. They were behind by six points.

☐   Steven had just saved a basket with a great block. But he had hurt his knee as he landed.

4   What is Steven's bold decision?

    Ⓐ   Deciding to play when he is hurt

    Ⓑ   Deciding to take the final shot

    Ⓒ   Deciding to win the game

    Ⓓ   Deciding to try to make a three point shot

5   Read this sentence from the passage.

He ignored the pain in his knee and sprinted forward.

The word <u>sprinted</u> shows that Steven moved –

    Ⓐ   quickly

    Ⓑ   shakily

    Ⓒ   quietly

    Ⓓ   slowly

6   Why does Steven decide to play?

    Ⓐ   He really wants his team to win.

    Ⓑ   He does not want to upset his coach.

    Ⓒ   He does not realize that he is hurt.

    Ⓓ   He wants everyone to cheer for him.

7   What is the last paragraph mainly about?

Ⓐ   How Steven's team won the game

Ⓑ   How Steven felt at the end of the game

Ⓒ   Why the game was important to Steven

Ⓓ   How to shoot a basket correctly

8   Based on your answer to Question 7, explain why the last paragraph is
important to the main idea of the story. Use **two** details from the passage
to support your response.

steven liked basketball.
he played basketball.

9   The author would probably describe Steven as –

Ⓐ   kind

Ⓑ   clever

Ⓒ   silly

Ⓓ   brave

10   Do you think Steven's team would have won if he had not of finished the
          game? Use **two** details from the passage to support your response.

_____

_____

_____

_____

_____

11   Read this paragraph from the passage.

> **Steven knew the risks of his decision. He could risk hurting his
> knee even more. Or he could choose not to play. He knew
> that not playing might cause his team to lose. As he rested
> before the final quarter, he decided to play through the pain.
> He was going to win this game for the team he loved.**

What do you learn about Steven from this paragraph?

_____

_____

_____

_____

_____

12   In the passage, Steven makes a decision for the good of his team. Do you think that Steven did the right thing by deciding to keep playing? Explain why or why not. Use details from the passage to support your response.

In your response, be sure to
- give your opinion on whether or not Steven did the right thing
- explain why you feel that way
- use details from the passage to support your answer

_____

_____

_____

_____

_____

_____

_____

_____

_____

_____

_____

_____

_____

END OF PRACTICE SET

Common Core ELA

Practice Set 13

Informational Text with MC, SR, and ER Questions

Instructions

This set has one passage for you to read. The passage is followed by questions.

Read each question carefully. For each multiple-choice question, fill in the circle for the correct answer. For other types of questions, follow the instructions given. Some of the questions require a written answer. Write your answer on the lines provided.

Rice Crispy Cakes

Rice crispy cakes are popular treats for children. Everybody loves how crunchy they are. The rice crispy and chocolate flavor is always a hit. And they are a perfect treat for sharing with friends. They are quick and easy to make too.

You only need a few simple things to make them. You will need some crispy rice cereal, butter, and a block of milk chocolate. You will also require a small bowl, a medium saucepan, a large saucepan, a baking tray, and patty cake holders.

What to Do

1. Start by pouring the crispy rice cereal into the small bowl.

2. Add 3 to 4 tablespoons of butter. It is a good idea to soften the butter first. Mix everything together with your hands. Just make sure you clean your hands first! You don't want to get dirt or germs through the mix.

3. You should now be able to fill the patty cake holders. Put a clump of the rice cereal mixture into each holder.

4. Next, you need to melt your block of chocolate. Fill a medium saucepan with water. Chop up about 2 ounces of chocolate. Place it in a small saucepan. Place the small saucepan in the medium saucepan. This will allow the hot water to gradually melt the bar of chocolate. Be careful you don't get water in with the chocolate. It will make the chocolate go hard and grainy. When your chocolate has turned to a thick liquid, it is ready to add to your crispy rice mixture.

5. Let the chocolate cool just enough so it does not burn you. Carefully pour a small amount of melted chocolate onto each ball of crispy rice. Make sure that each rice crispy cake is covered.

6. Arrange each crispy cake on the baking tray and place in the oven.

7. Bake them at 350 degrees for about 30 minutes.

8. When they're done baking, take them out of the oven and allow them to cool.

That's it! Your delicious treats are ready to enjoy or share!

****

1   In the sentence below, what does the word <u>gradually</u> most likely mean?

This will allow the hot water to gradually melt the bar of chocolate.

Ⓐ   Nicely

Ⓑ   Slowly

Ⓒ   Firmly

Ⓓ   Quickly

2   Read these sentences from the passage.

You will need some crispy rice cereal, butter, and a block of milk chocolate. You will also require a small bowl, a medium saucepan, a large saucepan, a baking tray, and patty cake holders.

What would the author be best to use to give this information more clearly?

Ⓐ   Map

Ⓑ   List

Ⓒ   Diagram

Ⓓ   Timeline

3   What is probably the main purpose of softening the butter?

Ⓐ   To make it easier to mix with the cereal

Ⓑ   To help the chocolate melt

Ⓒ   To make the rice crispy cake cook quicker

Ⓓ   To make it easier to measure out

4   What is the main purpose of the passage?

Ⓐ   To teach readers how to do something

Ⓑ   To entertain readers with a story

Ⓒ   To inform readers about crispy rice cereal

Ⓓ   To compare different types of sweets

5   In Step 3, what does the word <u>clump</u> show?

Ⓐ   Only a small amount of mixture should be used.

Ⓑ   The mixture does not have to be a perfect shape.

Ⓒ   The mixture is made of rice crispy cereal.

Ⓓ   The mixture should be a smooth round ball.

6   When are the patty cake holders first needed? Circle the correct step.

Step 1   Step 2   Step 3   Step 4

Step 5   Step 6   Step 7   Step 8

7   Which of these would most help the reader make the rice crispy cakes?

Ⓐ   A picture of a box of cereal

Ⓑ   A list of different types of cereals

Ⓒ   A photograph of a rice crispy cake

Ⓓ   A timeline of the events

8   Which step does the photograph most help the reader complete?

Ⓐ   Step 3

Ⓑ   Step 4

Ⓒ   Step 5

Ⓓ   Step 6

9   What type of passage is "Rice Crispy Cakes"?

Ⓐ   Recipe

Ⓑ   Essay

Ⓒ   Advertisement

Ⓓ   Letter

10   Think about your answer to Question 9. Describe **two** features of the passage that help show what type it is.

Feature 1:

_____

_____

Feature 2:

_____

_____

11   Choose **two** more reasons the author gives to show that rice crispy cakes are a good treat to make. Write the details in the chart below.

Rice crispy cakes are a good treat to make.

They are easy to share.

12   Choose **three** tasks to be done when making the rice crispy cakes where you would have to be careful. Explain why you have to be careful and what you should do to stop things going wrong. Use information from the passage to support your answer.

In your response, be sure to
- identify **three** tasks where you would need to be careful
- explain why you would have to be careful
- describe what you should do to stop things going wrong
- use details from the passage to support your answer

_____

_____

_____

_____

_____

_____

_____

_____

_____

_____

_____

END OF PRACTICE SET

Common Core ELA

Practice Set 14

Paired Informational Texts

Instructions

This set has two short passages for you to read. Read each passage and answer the questions that follow it.

For each multiple-choice question, fill in the circle for the correct answer. For other types of questions, follow the instructions given. Some of the questions require a written answer. Write your answer on the lines provided.

After reading both passages, you will use information from both passages to answer a question. Write your answer on the lines provided.

Nintendo

Did you know that Nintendo didn't always make video game consoles? Before the first Nintendo gaming console was ever thought of, Nintendo was making playing cards!

Nintendo was originally founded in 1889 to make playing cards for a game called Hanafuda. Nintendo later tried many different business ideas before finding its success. These included a taxi company, a television network, and a food company.

All of Nintendo's earlier business attempts eventually failed. It was not until 1983 when Nintendo launched the original Nintendo Entertainment System (NES) that the company found commercial success. A handheld game console called the Game Boy followed in 1989.

It has since gone on to make other similar products. The Nintendo DS was released in 2004 and has sold over 150 million units. The Nintendo Wii was launched in 2006. It was a gaming system that was able to sense the movements of players, and use the physical movements of the player to direct the game. For example, someone playing tennis would swing the controller to cause the player in the game to swing the tennis racket. The Wii sold over 90 million units in less than 5 years.

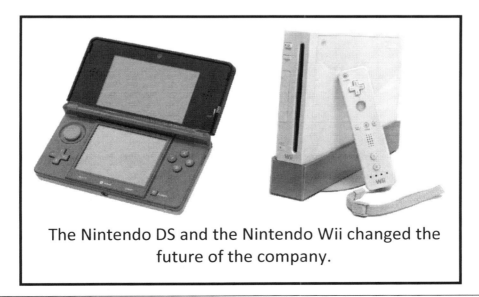

The Nintendo DS and the Nintendo Wii changed the future of the company.

1   The passage states that Nintendo did not find commercial success until 1983. Which word could best be used in place of <u>commercial</u>?

    Ⓐ   Business

    Ⓑ   Long-term

    Ⓒ   Sudden

    Ⓓ   Public

2   Why does the author begin the passage with a question?

    Ⓐ   To show that the information may not be true

    Ⓑ   To get readers interested in the topic of the passage

    Ⓒ   To suggest that readers should research the topic

    Ⓓ   To explain how Nintendo changed over the years

3   If the passage was given another title, which title would best fit?

    Ⓐ   The Future of Nintendo

    Ⓑ   How to Play Nintendo

    Ⓒ   Collecting Playing Cards

    Ⓓ   The Beginnings of a Business

4   The photographs are most likely included in the passage to –

    Ⓐ   provide examples of Nintendo's successful products

    Ⓑ   help readers understand what made Nintendo's products successful

    Ⓒ   demonstrate how important it was that Nintendo did not give up

    Ⓓ   show how the Nintendo Wii was different from other systems

5   Complete the web below using information from the passage.

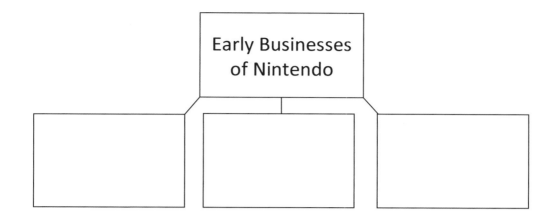

6   List the entertainment products created by Nintendo in the order they were created.

_____

_____

_____

_____

_____

_____

Breaking In

Today, Apple is a success in the personal computer market. It offers a range of effective and attractive products. But it wasn't always that way. Apple had to struggle to break into the market.

At the time, IBM was the leader in the market. Most people wanted to buy IBM computers, and very few wanted the Apple products. Then Apple introduced the iMac G3 in 1998. The iMac G3 was one of the first real successes for Apple. Previous to the iMac, Apple saw only limited success with its earlier desktop models.

The iMac G3 came after new Apple CEO Steve Jobs decided to trim Apple's product line. He decided to focus on making products that people would like. It was a bold move and an effective one. The striking design of the iMac was just one of the reasons it was special.

The iMac G3 was unlike any computer that had been seen. The computer parts were no longer in a separate case, but were part of the monitor. The computer now looked better and took up less space. It was first released in blue, but other bright colors were soon added. The color and style were an immediate hit. Unlike the drab computers others offered, the iMac looked bright and fun to use.

7   Read this sentence from the passage.

The iMac G3 came after new Apple CEO Steve Jobs decided to trim Apple's product line.

The word <u>trim</u> is used to show that Steve Jobs –

Ⓐ   made each product smaller

Ⓑ   reduced the number of products

Ⓒ   decreased the weight of the products

Ⓓ   made the products look more attractive

8   The author probably wrote this passage to –

Ⓐ   encourage people to buy Apple products

Ⓑ   describe a turning point for a company

Ⓒ   analyze the sales methods of a computer company

Ⓓ   tell about the life of Steve Jobs

9   Which sentence from the passage is a fact?

Ⓐ   *It offers a range of effective and attractive products.*

Ⓑ   *Then Apple introduced the iMac G3 in 1998.*

Ⓒ   *It was a bold move and an effective one.*

Ⓓ   *The striking design of the iMac was just one of the reasons it was special.*

10   Complete the table below by describing **two** ways the iMac G3 was different from other computers at the time.

Other Computers at the Time	The iMac G3

11   Read this sentence from the passage.

He decided to focus on making products that people would like.

Did the iMac G3 achieve this? Use **two** details from the passage to support your response.

_____

_____

_____

_____

_____

12   Think about what you learned about the companies Nintendo and Apple.
Describe how their histories are similar and how they are different. Use
details from **both** passages in your answer.

In your response, be sure to
- describe how the histories of Nintendo and Apple are similar
- describe how the histories of Nintendo and Apple are different
- use details from **both** passages to support your answer

_____

_____

_____

_____

_____

_____

_____

_____

_____

_____

_____

END OF PRACTICE SET

Common Core ELA

Practice Set 15

Informational Text with MC, SR, and ER Questions

Instructions
This set has one passage for you to read. The passage is followed by questions. Read each question carefully. For each multiple-choice question, fill in the circle for the correct answer. For other types of questions, follow the instructions given. Some of the questions require a written answer. Write your answer on the lines provided.

The New York Times

The New York Times is an American newspaper. It was founded in New York. It was first printed in 1851. The first issue cost just 1 cent to buy. It is printed each day. Each issue is read by around one million people. The newspaper has won over 110 Pulitzer Prizes. A Pulitzer Prize is an award given for excellent reporting. This is more than any other newspaper or magazine.

The New York Times is the largest local newspaper in the United States. It is also the third largest newspaper overall. Only *The Wall Street Journal* and *USA Today* are read by more people.

Even though it is still popular, it sells fewer copies today than in the past. In 1990, it was read by over a million people. By 2010, it was being read by less than a million people. This change has occurred for most printed newspapers. The main reason is that people can read the news on the Internet for free.

The newspaper's motto is "All the News That's Fit to Print." This appears printed in the top corner of the front page.

The newspaper has many different sections. It covers news, business, and science. It also covers sport, home, and fashion. It has sections for travel, food, art, and movies. It is also known for its difficult crossword puzzles.

In 2018, each issue sold for $2.50. However, the Sunday issue is larger. It is sold for $5 in New York or $6 in other parts of the United States.

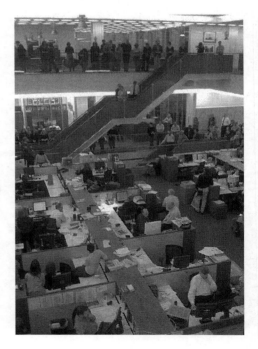

Hundreds of people work to create *The New York Times* every day.

1   Read this sentence from the passage.

It was founded in New York.

What does the word <u>founded</u> mean in the sentence?

Ⓐ   Sold

Ⓑ   Discovered

Ⓒ   Started

Ⓓ   Lost

2   Read this sentence from the passage.

The newspaper's motto is "All the News That's Fit to Print."

As it is used in this sentence, what does <u>fit</u> mean?

Ⓐ   Ready

Ⓑ   Healthy

Ⓒ   Right

Ⓓ   Known

3   According to the passage, how is *The Wall Street Journal* different from *The New York Times*?

    Ⓐ   It is read by more people.

    Ⓑ   It has won more awards.

    Ⓒ   It costs less to buy.

    Ⓓ   It has fewer sections.

4   According to the passage, why are fewer copies of *The New York Times* sold today than in the past?

    Ⓐ   It costs too much.

    Ⓑ   People read the news online.

    Ⓒ   People buy other newspapers instead.

    Ⓓ   It has too many sections.

5   Which word best describes the tone of the passage?

    Ⓐ   Gloomy

    Ⓑ   Serious

    Ⓒ   Lively

    Ⓓ   Hopeful

6   Which detail best shows that *The New York Times* is successful?

ⓐ   It is printed seven days a week.

ⓑ   Its price has increased to $2.50.

ⓒ   It has a motto.

ⓓ   It has won over 110 Pulitzer Prizes.

7   Use details from the passage to complete the web below.

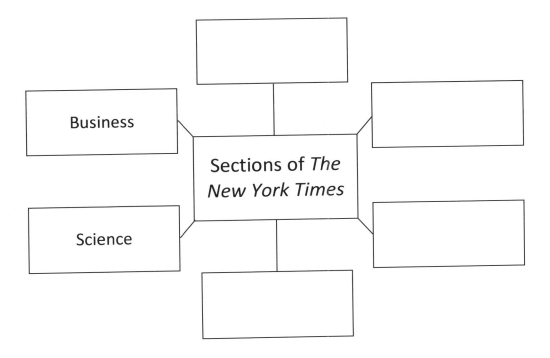

8   Read this sentence from the passage.

> **The main reason is that people can read the news on the Internet for free.**

In which sentence does <u>free</u> mean the same as in the sentence above?

Ⓐ   Jorja gave the kitten away for <u>free</u>.

Ⓑ   Andy was happy to have the whole day <u>free</u>.

Ⓒ   The diner was so busy that only one table was <u>free</u>.

Ⓓ   The beach always made Kyle feel relaxed and <u>free</u>.

9   Read this sentence from the passage.

> **The newspaper has won over 110 Pulitzer Prizes. A Pulitzer Prize is an award given for excellent reporting.**

Explain why the second sentence is important. In your answer, explain what the second sentence tells you about *The New York Times*.

_____

_____

_____

_____

_____

_____

10 Describe **two** things about *The New York Times* that have changed since it was first printed.

1: _____

_____

2: _____

_____

11 Which details from the passage did you find most interesting? Explain why you found those details interesting. Use **two** details from the passage to support your response.

_____

_____

_____

_____

_____

_____

12   The passage describes how many people today read the news on the
Internet. Explain why you think people choose to read the news online.
Explain how this trend is likely to affect newspapers like *The New York
Times*.

In your response, be sure to
- explain why you think people choose to read the news online
- describe at least two benefits of reading the news online
- explain how people reading the news online will affect newspapers
  like *The New York Times*
- use details from the passage to support your answer

_____

_____

_____

_____

_____

_____

_____

_____

_____

_____

_____

_____

_____

_____

_____

_____

_____

_____

_____

_____

_____

_____

_____

END OF PRACTICE SET

Common Core ELA

Practice Set 16

Literary Text with MC, SR, and ER Questions

Instructions

This set has one passage for you to read. The passage is followed by questions.

Read each question carefully. For each multiple-choice question, fill in the circle for the correct answer. For other types of questions, follow the instructions given. Some of the questions require a written answer. Write your answer on the lines provided.

Little Things
by Ebenezer Cobham Brewer

Little drops of water,
Little grains of sand,
Make the mighty ocean
And the pleasant land.

Thus the little minutes,
Humble though they be,
Make the mighty ages
Of eternity.

This canyon in Arizona is a popular place for tourists and adventure-seekers. People love to admire the view, take photographs, or raft along the Colorado River. It took millions of years for the canyon to form. As water flowed over the land, it wore away the rock little by little. Today, the result is a canyon that is thousands of feet deep.

1   In the lines below, what does the word <u>eternity</u> most likely mean?

**Make the mighty ages
Of eternity.**

Ⓐ   Time

Ⓑ   Forever

Ⓒ   Earth

Ⓓ   Everything

2   Read this line from the poem.

Make the mighty ocean

The word <u>mighty</u> suggests that the ocean is –

Ⓐ   strange

Ⓑ   scary

Ⓒ   powerful

Ⓓ   small

3   How many stanzas does the poem have? Circle the correct answer.

1   2   3   4   5   6   7   8

4   Which literary technique does the author use in the line below?

Make the mighty ages

Ⓐ   Alliteration

Ⓑ   Simile

Ⓒ   Metaphor

Ⓓ   Flashback

5   What is the rhyme pattern of each stanza of the poem?

Ⓐ   All the lines rhyme with each other.

Ⓑ   There are two pairs of rhyming lines.

Ⓒ   The second and fourth lines rhyme.

Ⓓ   None of the lines rhyme.

6   What are the lines below mainly about?

Thus the little minutes,
Humble though they be,
Make the mighty ages
Of eternity.

Ⓐ   Nature

Ⓑ   Earth

Ⓒ   Time

Ⓓ   Sleep

7   What is the main idea of the poem?

　　Ⓐ   Little things can form great things.

　　Ⓑ   Everything is always changing.

　　Ⓒ   Life could not survive without water.

　　Ⓓ   Time can go fast or slow.

8   Circle **all** the words that are repeated in the poem.

little   drops   mighty

water   sand   minutes

9   Explain how water, sand, and minutes are similar in the poem. Use **two** details from the passage to support your response.

_____

_____

_____

_____

_____

_____

10   Look at the picture of the canyon and read the caption. What idea does this show that is also a main idea in the poem? Use **two** details from the passage to support your response.

_____

_____

_____

_____

_____

_____

11   Based on your answer to Question 10, choose **two** details given in the caption that best show the main idea.

1: _____

_____

2: _____

_____

12   Just like how small grains of sand can create a large desert, small actions can create larger things over time. Think of an example from your life of how your small actions have led to something bigger over time. Describe what small actions you took and what they led to.

In your response, be sure to
- describe a time when small actions led to something bigger
- describe the small actions you took
- describe what happened because of the small actions you took

_____

_____

_____

_____

_____

_____

_____

_____

_____

_____

_____

_____

END OF PRACTICE SET

Common Core ELA

Practice Set 17

Informational Text with MC, SR, and ER Questions

Instructions
This set has one passage for you to read. The passage is followed by questions.
Read each question carefully. For each multiple-choice question, fill in the circle for the correct answer. For other types of questions, follow the instructions given. Some of the questions require a written answer. Write your answer on the lines provided.

The Shining Light Day Center

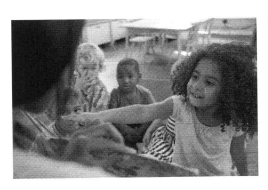

As parents, the wellbeing of your children is very important. It is important to keep them happy and healthy. It is also important to make sure their bodies and minds are active. It is especially important for children under the age of five. During this time, children can learn good fitness habits that they will keep for life.

During this time, children also learn quickly. They are at a special age where they take in information quickly. They also develop skills easier. It is important to find time to develop both their bodies and minds.

As parents, it can be hard to find time for all this. At the Shining Light Day Center, we understand this. We have created a range of activities to help your child.

Our activities cover many different areas. We want to help children think and learn. We want to help children learn to work with others. We want to help children learn to read and speak. We also want to help children be fit and healthy. Our activities include classes, games, and time for free play. These keep the child interested. At the same time, they are learning and growing.

Our programs are aimed at children between the ages of 3 and 5. Children will enjoy playing with others. They will learn basic math and English skills. Our program helps children start grade school. Think of it as a head start for your child!

Our classes are held at two different times. On weekdays, classes are held from noon to 3 p.m. On weekends, classes are held from 9 to 11 a.m. This gives you a lot of choice as a parent. You can choose the day and time that best suits you.

All parents should consider the Shining Light Day Center. It will give your child the best head start in life. Visit our website today to learn more. You can also call a member of our staff to discuss your child's future. You can also drop in any time to watch a class.

Learning Activity	Details
Storytelling	Children listen to stories being told. They answer questions about the story. Then they help write the ending to the story.
Telling Time	Students learn counting skills by using clocks. They count hours and minutes.
Hide and Seek	Children must find blocks hidden in our outdoor play areas. They race to find all the blocks of their color.
Puppet Show	Children use hand puppets to act out stories. They work in pairs.

1   Read this sentence from the passage.

They also develop skills easier.

Which word means the opposite of <u>easier</u>?

Ⓐ   Simpler

Ⓑ   Harder

Ⓒ   Quicker

Ⓓ   Slower

2   Which two words from the passage have about the same meaning?

Ⓐ   *read, speak*

Ⓑ   *fit, healthy*

Ⓒ   *day, time*

Ⓓ   *learning, school*

3   The passage is most like –

Ⓐ   an essay

Ⓑ   an advertisement

Ⓒ   a short story

Ⓓ   a news article

4   How is the third paragraph mainly organized?

    Ⓐ   A problem is described and then a solution is given.

    Ⓑ   Events are described in the order they occur.

    Ⓒ   Facts are given to support an argument.

    Ⓓ   A question is asked and then answered.

5   Read this sentence from the passage.

    You can also drop in any time to watch a class.

    What do the words "drop in" mean?

    Ⓐ   Phone

    Ⓑ   Check

    Ⓒ   Visit

    Ⓓ   Watch

6   The passage was probably written mainly to –

    Ⓐ   encourage parents to send their children to the day center

    Ⓑ   compare the day center with grade school

    Ⓒ   describe why the day center was started

    Ⓓ   inform parents about the benefits of learning

7   The web below describes the different areas covered by the activities.
     Complete the chart by listing **two** more areas covered by the activities.

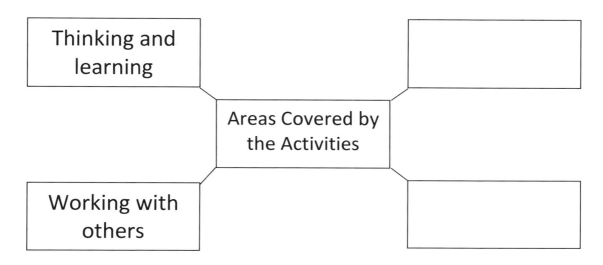

8   What do you think the author's main purpose for including the table is?
     Use **two** details from the passage to support your response.

_____

_____

_____

_____

_____

_____

9   Which sentence is included mainly to persuade the reader?

Ⓐ   *As parents, it can be hard to find time for all this.*

Ⓑ   *Our programs are aimed at children between the ages of 3 and 5.*

Ⓒ   *On weekdays, classes are held from noon to 3 p.m.*

Ⓓ   *It will give your child the best head start in life.*

10   Which activity from the table would be most likely to develop math skills?

Ⓐ   Storytelling

Ⓑ   Telling Time

Ⓒ   Hide and Seek

Ⓓ   Puppet Show

11   Read these sentences from the first paragraph.

> **It is also important to make sure their bodies and minds are active.
> It is especially important for children under the age of five.**

List **two** reasons the author gives to show why it is important for children under the age of five.

1: _____

_____

2: _____

_____

12   What do you think children would gain from going to the Shining Light Day Center? Describe at least **three** benefits to children of going to the Shining Light Day Center. Use details from the passage in your answer.

In your response, be sure to
- describe what children would gain from going to the day center
- include at least **three** benefits of going to the day center
- use details from the passage to support your answer

_____

_____

_____

_____

_____

_____

_____

_____

_____

_____

_____

_____

_____

END OF PRACTICE SET

Common Core ELA

Practice Set 18

Paired Literary Texts

Instructions

This set has two short passages for you to read. Read each passage and answer the questions that follow it.

For each multiple-choice question, fill in the circle for the correct answer. For other types of questions, follow the instructions given. Some of the questions require a written answer. Write your answer on the lines provided.

After reading both passages, you will use information from both passages to answer a question. Write your answer on the lines provided.

Vacation Time

Quinn, Harley, and Max were sitting beside the basketball court eating lunch.

"What are you doing this summer, Harley?" Quinn asked.

"Well, I'll probably go to see my grandparents in Florida," Harley replied. "What about you?"

"That sounds like fun. I'm probably going to go visit my Dad in Australia!" Quinn said.

"What about you?" Quinn asked Max.

"I'm going to stay here in town," Max said.

Quinn and Harley both shook their heads sadly.

"Well, that sounds awfully boring," Harley said.

Max tilted his head a little and thought for a moment.

"Well, I'm going to watch television, play basketball, go to the local swimming pool, ride my bike, play computer games, read some books..."

Max went on and on and listed even more things he was going to do.

Quinn stared at Max, "Oh boy, is that all?"

The boys laughed and ate the rest of their lunch.

1 Which statement is most likely true about Max?

Ⓐ He wishes he could visit Australia.

Ⓑ He is looking forward to summer.

Ⓒ He thinks summer will be boring.

Ⓓ He wants his friends to stay in town.

2 What is the passage mainly about?

Ⓐ Three boys discussing their vacations

Ⓑ Three boys trying to think of something fun to do

Ⓒ Three boys playing basketball together

Ⓓ Three boys arguing about what to do together

3 In which sentence from the passage is the character being humorous?

Ⓐ *"What are you doing this summer, Harley?" Quinn asked.*

Ⓑ *"I'm going to stay here in town," Max said.*

Ⓒ *"Well, that sounds awfully boring," Harley said.*

Ⓓ *Quinn stared at Max, "Oh boy, is that all?"*

4 What does the photograph in the passage represent?

Ⓐ What Quinn and Harley will miss most when they are away

Ⓑ Where the boys are talking about their summers

Ⓒ How you can do fun things on your own

Ⓓ One of the things Max plans to do over summer

5   How are Max's vacation plans different from Quinn's and Hoy's? Use **two** details from the passage to support your response.

_____

_____

_____

_____

_____

6   Do you think that Max's vacation plans sound interesting or dull? Use **two** details from the passage to support your response.

_____

_____

_____

_____

_____

Fish Food

"Come on, it's not that far now!" Sam yelled.

Ben wiped away some sweat and kept going. It was a very warm day, and it just kept getting warmer.

Sam and Ben were on their way to the big lake to catch some fish. They had their fishing rods and some bait to put on their hooks.

They finally found a good spot near the lake. They sat down to start fishing. Ben opened the ice cream container where he had asked his mother to put the bait.

"This is not fishing bait. These worms are made of candy!" Ben said. "I should have told Mom I wanted worms to use as bait."

"We could still try," Sam offered. "Maybe the fish will like the candy worms."

Ben wasn't sure it would work, but it sounded like fun. He didn't mind if they didn't catch anything anyway. He just liked sitting back and enjoying a lazy afternoon by the lake.

"It's worth a try," Ben said. "But we should keep a few worms for ourselves."

7   What will Sam and Ben most likely do next?

  Ⓐ   Start eating the candy worms

  Ⓑ   Start fishing using the candy worms

  Ⓒ   Choose a different spot to fish

  Ⓓ   Decide to go home and do something else

8   What is the most likely reason Ben's mother put candy in the ice cream container?

  Ⓐ   She thought that they would make good bait.

  Ⓑ   She didn't realize that Ben wanted worms for bait.

  Ⓒ   She didn't want Sam and Ben to catch any fish.

  Ⓓ   She wanted Sam and Ben to have a snack to eat.

9   What happens right after Ben opens the ice cream container?

  Ⓐ   He sees that he has candy worms.

  Ⓑ   He finds a good fishing spot.

  Ⓒ   He decides to fish anyway.

  Ⓓ   He asks his mother to pack the bait.

10   The photograph in the passage mainly makes the lake seem like –

  Ⓐ   a busy place

  Ⓑ   an exciting place

  Ⓒ   a peaceful place

  Ⓓ   a lonely place

11　The setting of a story is where and when it takes place. Complete the table below by stating what you think the setting is in the second column. In the last column, describe the detail from the story that helped you decide what the setting was.

	Setting	Supporting Details
Where the story takes place		
What time of day the story takes place		
What time of year the story takes place		

12   Max and Sam can both be described as characters that make the most out
of things. Explain how you can tell that Max and Sam both like to make the
most out of things. Use details from **both** passages in your answer.

In your response, be sure to
- describe how you can tell that Max makes the most out of things
- describe how you can tell that Sam makes the most out of things
- use details from **both** passages to support your answer

_____

_____

_____

_____

_____

_____

_____

_____

_____

_____

_____

_____

END OF PRACTICE SET

ANSWER KEY

English Language Arts Learning Standards

In 2017, the state of New York introduced the Next Generation Learning Standards. These are revised standards that replace the previous Common Core Learning Standards, though remain very close in content. State testing will continue to assess the Common Core Learning Standards until 2020, but the new standards will be gradually implemented over this time. This workbook has aligned all questions to the new Next Generation Learning Standards. However, the questions still also cover the Common Core standards that are assessed on the state tests.

Reading Standards

The majority of the questions assess reading standards. The reading standards are divided into the following two areas:

- Reading Standards for Literary Text
- Reading Standards for Informational Text

Within each of these areas, there are nine standards that describe specific skills the student should have. The answer key on the following pages lists the standard assessed by each question. The skill listed can be used to identify a student's areas of strength and weakness, so revision and instruction can be targeted accordingly.

Scoring Short-Response and Extended-Response Questions

This workbook includes short-response and extended-response questions, where students provide a written answer to a question. Short-response questions assess reading skills and are scored out of 2. The answer key gives guidance on how to score these questions and lists what should be included in the answer.

Extended-response questions assess both reading and writing skills. A 4-point rubric is used to give an overall score out of 4 based on four considerations. The rubric used for scoring these questions is included in the back of this book. Use the rubric to score these questions, and as a guide for giving the student advice on how to improve an answer.

Practice Set 1

Question	Answer	Next Generation Learning Standard
1	A	Determine the meaning of words, phrases, figurative language, and academic and content-specific words.
2	C	Determine the meaning of words, phrases, figurative language, and academic and content-specific words.
3	See Below	Develop and answer questions to locate relevant and specific details in a text to support an answer or inference.
4	D	Determine a theme or central idea and explain how it is supported by key details; summarize portions of a text.
5	A	Determine a theme or central idea and explain how it is supported by key details; summarize portions of a text.
6	C	Determine the meaning of words, phrases, figurative language, and academic and content-specific words.
7	D	Recognize genres and make connections to other texts, ideas, cultural perspectives, eras, personal events, and situations.
8	B	In literary texts, describe character traits, motivations, or feelings, drawing on specific details from the text.
9	A	In literary texts, describe character traits, motivations, or feelings, drawing on specific details from the text.
10	C	Determine a theme or central idea and explain how it is supported by key details; summarize portions of a text.
11	See Below	Determine a theme or central idea and explain how it is supported by key details; summarize portions of a text.
12	See Below	Discuss how the reader's point of view or perspective may differ from that of the author, narrator or characters in a text.

Q3.
Give a score of 0, 1, or 2 based on how well the answer meets the criteria listed below.
- The web should be completed with three examples from the passage of things that Sarah and Janet compete over.
- Answers include singing, running fast, playing volleyball, reading fast, and choosing clothes.

Q11.
Give a score of 0, 1, or 2 based on how well the answer meets the criteria listed below.
- It should give a reasonable explanation of why the student chose the title.
- It should relate the title to the theme of the passage.
- It should use relevant details from the passage.

Q12.
Give a score of 0, 1, or 2 based on how well the answer meets the criteria listed below.
- It should give a reasonable description of how the girls competing could be good for them.
- The answer may refer to how it makes the girls try harder or how it encourages them to do better.

Practice Set 2

Question	Answer	Next Generation Learning Standard
1	C	Determine the meaning of words, phrases, figurative language, and academic and content-specific words.
2	B	In literary texts, describe character traits, motivations, or feelings, drawing on specific details from the text.
3	D	In literary texts, describe character traits, motivations, or feelings, drawing on specific details from the text.
4	See Below	Explain how claims in a text are supported by relevant reasons and evidence.
5	A	Determine the meaning of words, phrases, figurative language, and academic and content-specific words.
6	D	Discuss how the reader's point of view or perspective may differ from that of the author, narrator or characters in a text.
7	B	Determine a theme or central idea and explain how it is supported by key details; summarize portions of a text.
8	C	Determine the meaning of words, phrases, figurative language, and academic and content-specific words.
9	afraid brave	In literary texts, describe character traits, motivations, or feelings, drawing on specific details from the text.
10	See Below	Discuss how the reader's point of view or perspective may differ from that of the author, narrator or characters in a text.
11	See Below	Determine a theme or central idea and explain how it is supported by key details; summarize portions of a text.
12	See Below	Write informative/explanatory texts to explore a topic and convey ideas and information relevant to the subject.

Q4.
Give a score of 0, 1, or 2 based on how many relevant details are listed. Possible answers are listed below.

- He is quiet as they drive into the city. / He gasps when he looks up at the tower. / His stomach turns over. / He says that he's not sure if he can do it. / He takes a deep breath as he steps through the entrance. / He holds his father's hand.

Q10.
Give a score of 0, 1, or 2 based on how well the answer meets the criteria listed below.

- It should make a reasonable inference about how Toby feels at the end of the passage.
- The inference could be that he feels proud of himself, unafraid, or relieved.
- It should use relevant details from the passage.

Q11.
Give a score of 0, 1, or 2 based on how well the answer meets the criteria listed below.

- It should identify Toby's problem as that he has a fear of heights.
- It should describe how Toby faces his fear by climbing to the top of the Eiffel Tower.
- It should use relevant details from the passage.

Q12. Use the 4-point rubric at the end of the answer key to give an overall score of 0, 1, 2, 3, or 4.

Practice Set 3

Question	Answer	Next Generation Learning Standard
1	D	Determine the meaning of words, phrases, figurative language, and academic and content-specific words.
2	C	In informational texts, describe the relationship among a series of events, ideas, concepts, or steps in a text, using language that pertains to time, sequence, and cause/effect.
3	B	Determine a theme or central idea and explain how it is supported by key details; summarize portions of a text.
4	A	Determine the meaning of words, phrases, figurative language, and academic and content-specific words.
5	C	In informational texts, identify and use text features to build comprehension.
6	B	Develop and answer questions to locate relevant and specific details in a text to support an answer or inference.
7	B	Explain how specific illustrations or text features contribute to what is conveyed by the words in a text.
8	"suggest a lower price"	Determine the meaning of words, phrases, figurative language, and academic and content-specific words.
9	See Below	Explain how specific illustrations or text features contribute to what is conveyed by the words in a text.
10	See Below	Explain how claims in a text are supported by relevant reasons and evidence.
11	See Below	Discuss how the reader's point of view or perspective may differ from that of the author, narrator or characters in a text.
12	See Below	In informational texts, describe the relationship among a series of events, ideas, concepts, or steps in a text, using language that pertains to time, sequence, and cause/effect.

Q9.
Give a score of 0, 1, or 2 based on how many relevant examples are given.
- Any reasonable answer can be accepted as long as it relates the art to passage content.
- The answer could refer to the items shown, the table, or the poster.

Q10.
Give a score of 0.5 for each sentence correctly matched with its purpose. The correct matches are listed below.
- A yard sale is when you sell items in your front yard. → to tell what a yard sale is
- People have yard sales to get rid of unwanted items. → to give the main reason for having a yard sale
- It can also be a good way to make some extra money. → to give a second reason for having a yard sale
- Here are some tips on how to have a good yard sale. → to tell what the passage is about

Q11.
Give a score of 0, 1, or 2 based on how well the answer meets the criteria listed below.
- It should give a reasonable explanation of why asking other people to join in would be a good idea.
- The benefits may include having more items to sell, having help to run it, or making more money.

Q12.
Give a score of 1 for each column completed correctly. The correct matches are listed below.
- The Week Before Your Yard Sale → put up flyers, tell your friends, run a newspaper ad
- On the Day of Your Yard Sale → put balloons up, set up the tables, put a sign in your street

Practice Set 4

Question	Answer	Next Generation Learning Standard
1	C	Determine the meaning of words, phrases, figurative language, and academic and content-specific words.
2	A	In informational texts, identify and use text features to build comprehension.
3	A	Determine a theme or central idea and explain how it is supported by key details; summarize portions of a text.
4	Step 1	In informational texts, describe the relationship among a series of events, ideas, concepts, or steps in a text, using language that pertains to time, sequence, and cause/effect.
5	B	Determine the meaning of words, phrases, figurative language, and academic and content-specific words.
6	See Below	In informational texts, describe the relationship among a series of events, ideas, concepts, or steps in a text, using language that pertains to time, sequence, and cause/effect.
7	C	Develop and answer questions to locate relevant and specific details in a text to support an answer or inference.
8	B	Explain how claims in a text are supported by relevant reasons and evidence.
9	See Below	Determine a theme or central idea and explain how it is supported by key details; summarize portions of a text.
10	See Below	In informational texts, describe the relationship among a series of events, ideas, concepts, or steps in a text, using language that pertains to time, sequence, and cause/effect.
11	See Below	Discuss how the reader's point of view or perspective may differ from that of the author, narrator or characters in a text.
12	See Below	Write informative/explanatory texts to explore a topic and convey ideas and information relevant to the subject.

Q6.
Give a score of 0, 1, or 2 based on how well the answer meets the criteria listed below.
- The diagram should be completed with each sentence in the correct place, as below.
- It is too sour. → Add sugar. / It is too sweet. → Add lemon juice. / It is too strong. → Add water.

Q9.
Give a score of 0, 1, or 2 based on how many relevant examples are given.
- Any reasonable answer can be accepted as long as it is based on information in the passage.
- The student may refer to setting up a lemonade at the friend's house, having help to make the lemonade, having someone to help decorate the stand, or selling other products the friend makes.

Q10.
The student should complete the chart in the order below. Give a score of 0.5 for each item correctly ordered.
- sugar → boiling water → lemon juice → cold water

Q11.
Give a score of 0, 1, or 2 based on how well the answer meets the criteria listed below.
- It should state whether or not the student feels it would be worth it to make lemonade.
- It should provide a fully-supported explanation of why or why not.

Q12. Use the 4-point rubric at the end of the answer key to give an overall score of 0, 1, 2, 3, or 4.

Practice Set 5

Question	Answer	Next Generation Learning Standard
1	B	In literary texts, describe character traits, motivations, or feelings, drawing on specific details from the text.
2	C	Develop and answer questions to locate relevant and specific details in a text to support an answer or inference.
3	B	In literary texts, identify parts of stories, dramas, and poems using terms such as chapter, scene, and stanza.
4	A	Discuss how the reader's point of view or perspective may differ from that of the author, narrator or characters in a text.
5	B	Develop and answer questions to locate relevant and specific details in a text to support an answer or inference.
6	See Below	Explain how claims in a text are supported by relevant reasons and evidence.
7	D	Develop and answer questions to locate relevant and specific details in a text to support an answer or inference.
8	B	Determine the meaning of words, phrases, figurative language, and academic and content-specific words.
9	B	Develop and answer questions to locate relevant and specific details in a text to support an answer or inference.
10	C	Explain how specific illustrations or text features contribute to what is conveyed by the words in a text.
11	See Below	In literary texts, describe character traits, motivations, or feelings, drawing on specific details from the text.
12	See Below	Write informative/explanatory texts to explore a topic and convey ideas and information relevant to the subject.

Q6.
Give a score of 0, 1, or 2 based on how many relevant details are given.
- Possible details could refer to how she paces up and down, how she keeps asking where he is, how she searches the crowd, or how she stands tall to try to see every person coming through the gate.

Q11.
Give a score of 0, 1, or 2 based on how well the answer meets the criteria listed below.
- It should provide a reasonable analysis of what the father's actions show about how he feels.
- It may refer to how he drops his bags or to how he sweeps his daughters into his arms.
- It should describe how he feels excited, overjoyed, or relieved.

Q12. Use the 4-point rubric at the end of the answer key to give an overall score of 0, 1, 2, 3, or 4.

Practice Set 6

Question	Answer	Next Generation Learning Standard
1	B	Determine the meaning of words, phrases, figurative language, and academic and content-specific words.
2	amazing beautiful	Discuss how the reader's point of view or perspective may differ from that of the author, narrator or characters in a text.
3	A	In literary texts, identify parts of stories, dramas, and poems using terms such as chapter, scene, and stanza.
4	C	Determine the meaning of words, phrases, figurative language, and academic and content-specific words.
5	B	Develop and answer questions to locate relevant and specific details in a text to support an answer or inference.
6	See Below	Determine the meaning of words, phrases, figurative language, and academic and content-specific words.
7	See Below	Develop and answer questions to locate relevant and specific details in a text to support an answer or inference.
8	See Below	Discuss how the reader's point of view or perspective may differ from that of the author, narrator or characters in a text.
9	See Below	Develop and answer questions to locate relevant and specific details in a text to support an answer or inference.
10	C	Determine a theme or central idea and explain how it is supported by key details; summarize portions of a text.

Q6.
Give a score of 0, 1, or 2 based on how lines are correctly selected. The correct lines are listed below.
- "with slow and steady ease" and "in the earth all wet and warm."

Q7.
Give a score of 0, 1, or 2 based on how well the answer meets the criteria listed below.
- It should give a reasonable explanation of how a worm is like an explorer.
- It should include a description of how worms explore under the ground.
- It should use relevant details from the poem.

Q8.
Give a score of 0, 1, or 2 based on how well the answer meets the criteria listed below.
- It should give an opinion on whether the poet is successful at showing readers that worms are interesting and special.
- It should provide a fully-supported explanation to support the opinion.

Q9.
Give a score of 0, 1, or 2 based on how well the answer meets the criteria listed below.
- It should show an understanding that the worm has a simple form or a "single beautiful shape."
- It should use relevant details from the poem.

Practice Set 7

Question	Answer	Next Generation Learning Standard
1	C	Develop and answer questions to locate relevant and specific details in a text to support an answer or inference.
2	A	Determine the meaning of words, phrases, figurative language, and academic and content-specific words.
3	C	In literary texts, identify parts of stories, dramas, and poems using terms such as chapter, scene, and stanza.
4	C	Determine the meaning of words, phrases, figurative language, and academic and content-specific words.
5	D	Determine the meaning of words, phrases, figurative language, and academic and content-specific words.
6	D	Determine a theme or central idea and explain how it is supported by key details; summarize portions of a text.
7	See Below	Explain how specific illustrations or text features contribute to what is conveyed by the words in a text.
8	See Below	Develop and answer questions to locate relevant and specific details in a text to support an answer or inference.
9	See Below	Develop and answer questions to locate relevant and specific details in a text to support an answer or inference.
10	See Below	Write informative/explanatory texts to explore a topic and convey ideas and information relevant to the subject.

Q7.
Give a score of 0, 1, or 2 based on how well the answer meets the criteria listed below.
- It should provide a reasonable description of what the photograph helps readers understand.
- The answer could refer to how the photograph shows how bees make honey or to how it shows how beekeepers protect themselves.

Q8.
Give a score of 0, 1, or 2 based on how well the answer meets the criteria listed below.
- The web should be completed with three facts from the passage about bees.
- Any detail included in the poem or caption can be accepted as long as it is factual and not an opinion.

Q9.
Give a score of 0, 1, or 2 based on how well the answer meets the criteria listed below.
- It should provide a reasonable explanation of whether or not people need to fear bees. Either answer is acceptable as long as it is supported.
- The answer may refer to how bees do not wish to harm, how bees usually only sting when they are afraid, or how leaving bees alone keeps you safe from them.
- The answer may refer to how many bees can be dangerous or how beekeepers need to wear safety suits.

Q10. Use the 4-point rubric at the end of the answer key to give an overall score of 0, 1, 2, 3, or 4.

Practice Set 8

Question	Answer	Next Generation Learning Standard
1	A	Determine the meaning of words, phrases, figurative language, and academic and content-specific words.
2	A	Determine the meaning of words, phrases, figurative language, and academic and content-specific words.
3	D	In informational texts, describe the relationship among a series of events, ideas, concepts, or steps in a text, using language that pertains to time, sequence, and cause/effect.
4	See Below	Explain how claims in a text are supported by relevant reasons and evidence.
5	See Below	In informational texts, identify and use text features to build comprehension.
6	C	Develop and answer questions to locate relevant and specific details in a text to support an answer or inference.
7	A	Determine a theme or central idea and explain how it is supported by key details; summarize portions of a text.
8	C	In informational texts, identify and use text features to build comprehension.
9	See Below	Develop and answer questions to locate relevant and specific details in a text to support an answer or inference.
10	See Below	Discuss how the reader's point of view or perspective may differ from that of the author, narrator or characters in a text.

Q4.
Give a score of 0, 1, or 2 based on how well the answer meets the criteria listed below.
- Any of the last 4 sentences can be accepted.
- The student should provide a reasonable explanation of why the two sentences were chosen and how they show the reason for writing the letter.

Q5.
Give a score of 1 for each book added to the table correctly. The correct books are listed below.
- Favorite Book: *The Shining Light*
- First Book Read: *The Singing Swordfish*

Q9.
Give a score of 0, 1, or 2 based on how many relevant reasons are given.
- Possible reasons include that it was well-written, that the pictures were good, or that it made him laugh.

Q10.
Give a score of 0, 1, or 2 based on how well the answer meets the criteria listed below.
- It should give an opinion on whether or not Simeon would feel good after reading the letter.
- It should provide a fully-supported explanation to support the opinion.

Practice Set 9

Question	Answer	Next Generation Learning Standard
1	C	Determine the meaning of words, phrases, figurative language, and academic and content-specific words.
2	B	Determine the meaning of words, phrases, figurative language, and academic and content-specific words.
3	C	Develop and answer questions to locate relevant and specific details in a text to support an answer or inference.
4	A	Determine a theme or central idea and explain how it is supported by key details; summarize portions of a text.
5	D	Determine a theme or central idea and explain how it is supported by key details; summarize portions of a text.
6	A	Explain how claims in a text are supported by relevant reasons and evidence.
7	Standing up for yourself	In informational texts, identify and use text features to build comprehension.
8	C	Discuss how the reader's point of view or perspective may differ from that of the author, narrator or characters in a text.
9	See Below	Determine a theme or central idea and explain how it is supported by key details; summarize portions of a text.
10	See Below	Write informative/explanatory texts to explore a topic and convey ideas and information relevant to the subject.

Q9.
Give a score of 0, 1, or 2 based on how well the answer meets the criteria listed below.
- It should describe the benefits of increasing the length of the lunch break.
- The benefits described should be based on the argument from the passage.
- It should use relevant details from the passage.

Q10. Use the 4-point rubric at the end of the answer key to give an overall score of 0, 1, 2, 3, or 4.

Practice Set 10

Question	Answer	Next Generation Learning Standard
1	C	Determine the meaning of words, phrases, figurative language, and academic and content-specific words.
2	famous well-known	Determine the meaning of words, phrases, figurative language, and academic and content-specific words.
3	A	In literary texts, describe character traits, motivations, or feelings, drawing on specific details from the text.
4	B	Develop and answer questions to locate relevant and specific details in a text to support an answer or inference.
5	From top to bottom: 3, 2, 4, 1	In literary texts, identify parts of stories, dramas, and poems using terms such as chapter, scene, and stanza.
6	B	Determine a theme or central idea and explain how it is supported by key details; summarize portions of a text.
7	C	In literary texts, identify parts of stories, dramas, and poems using terms such as chapter, scene, and stanza.
8	D	In literary texts, describe character traits, motivations, or feelings, drawing on specific details from the text.
9	Sentences 3 and 4	Develop and answer questions to locate relevant and specific details in a text to support an answer or inference.
10	See Below	Determine a theme or central idea and explain how it is supported by key details; summarize portions of a text.
11	See Below	In literary texts, describe character traits, motivations, or feelings, drawing on specific details from the text.
12	See Below	Write informative/explanatory texts to explore a topic and convey ideas and information relevant to the subject.

Q10.
Give a score of 0, 1, or 2 based on how well the answer meets the criteria listed below.
- It should describe the lesson that Kevin learns in the story. The lesson should be not to be mean to others, to focus on being known for something positive, or how being funny can become nasty.
- It should use relevant details from the passage.

Q11.
Give a score of 0, 1, or 2 based on how well the answer meets the criteria listed below.
- It should make a prediction about whether or not Kevin will keep playing jokes.
- It should provide a fully-supported explanation to support the prediction.
- It should use relevant details from the passage.

Q12. Use the 4-point rubric at the end of the answer key to give an overall score of 0, 1, 2, 3, or 4.

Practice Set 11

Question	Answer	Next Generation Learning Standard
1	C	Determine the meaning of words, phrases, figurative language, and academic and content-specific words.
2	A	Determine the meaning of words, phrases, figurative language, and academic and content-specific words.
3	B	Develop and answer questions to locate relevant and specific details in a text to support an answer or inference.
4	A	Explain how claims in a text are supported by relevant reasons and evidence.
5	B	Determine a theme or central idea and explain how it is supported by key details; summarize portions of a text.
6	C	Determine a theme or central idea and explain how it is supported by key details; summarize portions of a text.
7	See Below	Develop and answer questions to locate relevant and specific details in a text to support an answer or inference.
8	B	In informational texts, describe the relationship among a series of events, ideas, concepts, or steps in a text, using language that pertains to time, sequence, and cause/effect.
9	B	Discuss how the reader's point of view or perspective may differ from that of the author, narrator or characters in a text.
10	D	Determine the meaning of words, phrases, figurative language, and academic and content-specific words.
11	See Below	In informational texts, describe the relationship among a series of events, ideas, concepts, or steps in a text, using language that pertains to time, sequence, and cause/effect.
12	See Below	Write informative/explanatory texts to explore a topic and convey ideas and information relevant to the subject.

Q7.
Give a score of 0, 1, or 2 based on how well the answer meets the criteria listed below.
- The second and third sentences should be circled.
- Any factual detail from the passage can be accepted.

Q11.
Give a score of 0, 1, or 2 based on how well the answer meets the criteria listed below.
- It should provide a reasonable explanation of why the 2008 Wimbledon final was important.
- It should include two reasons that the final was important. Possible reasons could refer to how Nadal stopped Roger from winning six times, how it was a tough match, how it started a row between them, or how some people think it was the best match ever played.

Q12. Use the 4-point rubric at the end of the answer key to give an overall score of 0, 1, 2, 3, or 4.

Practice Set 12

Question	Answer	Next Generation Learning Standard
1	B	Determine the meaning of words, phrases, figurative language, and academic and content-specific words.
2	decision choice	Determine the meaning of words, phrases, figurative language, and academic and content-specific words.
3	third pair	Develop and answer questions to locate relevant and specific details in a text to support an answer or inference.
4	A	Determine a theme or central idea and explain how it is supported by key details; summarize portions of a text.
5	A	Determine the meaning of words, phrases, figurative language, and academic and content-specific words.
6	A	In literary texts, describe character traits, motivations, or feelings, drawing on specific details from the text.
7	A	In literary texts, identify parts of stories, dramas, and poems using terms such as chapter, scene, and stanza.
8	See Below	Determine a theme or central idea and explain how it is supported by key details; summarize portions of a text.
9	D	Discuss how the reader's point of view or perspective may differ from that of the author, narrator or characters in a text.
10	See Below	In literary texts, describe character traits, motivations, or feelings, drawing on specific details from the text.
11	See Below	In literary texts, identify parts of stories, dramas, and poems using terms such as chapter, scene, and stanza.
12	See Below	Write an argument to support claim(s), using clear reasons and relevant evidence.

Q8.
Give a score of 0, 1, or 2 based on how well the answer meets the criteria listed below.
- It should provide a reasonable explanation of why the last paragraph is important to the main idea.
- The answer should refer to how the last paragraph shows that Steven's bold decision paid off.

Q10.
Give a score of 0, 1, or 2 based on how well the answer meets the criteria listed below.
- It should make a reasonable prediction about whether Steven team's would have won without him.
- Any prediction can be accepted as long as it is explained and supported with details from the passage.

Q11.
Give a score of 0, 1, or 2 based on how well the answer meets the criteria listed below.
- It should provide an analysis of what the paragraph reveals about Steven.
- The answer may refer to how it shows that he knew playing was a risk to himself, how he thought carefully about his decision, or how he put the needs of his team first.

Q12. Use the 4-point rubric at the end of the answer key to give an overall score of 0, 1, 2, 3, or 4.

Practice Set 13

Question	Answer	Next Generation Learning Standard
1	B	Determine the meaning of words, phrases, figurative language, and academic and content-specific words.
2	B	In informational texts, identify and use text features to build comprehension.
3	A	In informational texts, describe the relationship among a series of events, ideas, concepts, or steps in a text, using language that pertains to time, sequence, and cause/effect.
4	A	Determine a theme or central idea and explain how it is supported by key details; summarize portions of a text.
5	B	Determine the meaning of words, phrases, figurative language, and academic and content-specific words.
6	Step 3	In informational texts, describe the relationship among a series of events, ideas, concepts, or steps in a text, using language that pertains to time, sequence, and cause/effect.
7	C	Explain how specific illustrations or text features contribute to what is conveyed by the words in a text.
8	B	Explain how specific illustrations or text features contribute to what is conveyed by the words in a text.
9	A	Recognize genres and make connections to other texts, ideas, cultural perspectives, eras, personal events, and situations.
10	See Below	Recognize genres and make connections to other texts, ideas, cultural perspectives, eras, personal events, and situations.
11	See Below	Explain how claims in a text are supported by relevant reasons and evidence.
12	See Below	Write informative/explanatory texts to explore a topic and convey ideas and information relevant to the subject.

Q10.
Give a score of 0, 1, or 2 based on how many acceptable features are listed.
- Any feature that helps show that the passage is a recipe can be accepted.
- The features could be broad, such as that the passage tells how to make a food or gives directions.
- The features could be specific, such as that the passage has a section titled "What to Do," has steps to follow, or includes a picture of making food.

Q11.
Give a score of 0, 1, or 2 based on how many correct reasons are given.
- Possible answers include that children like them, that they are crunchy, that the flavor is a hit, or that they are easy to make.

Q12. Use the 4-point rubric at the end of the answer key to give an overall score of 0, 1, 2, 3, or 4.
- The three tasks identified could be based on softening the butter in step 2, cleaning your hands before mixing in step 2, not getting water in the chocolate in step 4, letting the chocolate cool in step 5, or making sure the rice crispy cake is covered in chocolate in step 5.

Practice Set 14

Question	Answer	Next Generation Learning Standard
1	A	Determine the meaning of words, phrases, figurative language, and academic and content-specific words.
2	B	Discuss how the reader's point of view or perspective may differ from that of the author, narrator or characters in a text.
3	D	Determine a theme or central idea and explain how it is supported by key details; summarize portions of a text.
4	A	Explain how specific illustrations or text features contribute to what is conveyed by the words in a text.
5	See Below	Develop and answer questions to locate relevant and specific details in a text to support an answer or inference.
6	See Below	In informational texts, describe the relationship among a series of events, ideas, concepts, or steps in a text, using language that pertains to time, sequence, and cause/effect.
7	B	Determine the meaning of words, phrases, figurative language, and academic and content-specific words.
8	B	Determine a theme or central idea and explain how it is supported by key details; summarize portions of a text.
9	B	Develop and answer questions to locate relevant and specific details in a text to support an answer or inference.
10	See Below	In informational texts, identify and use text features to build comprehension.
11	See Below	Develop and answer questions to locate relevant and specific details in a text to support an answer or inference.
12	See Below	Recognize genres and make connections to other texts, ideas, cultural perspectives, eras, personal events, and situations.

Q5.
Give a score of 0, 1, or 2 based on how well the answer meets the criteria listed below.
- The web should be completed with three early businesses of Nintendo.
- The early businesses are maker of playing cards, taxi company, television network, and food company.

Q6.
Give a score of 0, 1, or 2 based on how well the answer meets the criteria listed below.
- It should list the entertainment products released by Nintendo in order from earliest to most recent.
- The products released in order from earliest to latest are: Nintendo Entertainment System (1983); Game Boy (1989); Nintendo DS (2004); and Nintendo Wii (2006).

Q10.
Give a score of 0, 1, or 2 based on how many correct comparisons are given.
- The answer may describe how other computers had their parts in a separate case while the iMac G3 had its parts in the monitor, how other computers were drab colors while the iMac G3 was bright, how the style of the iMac G3 was liked more, or how the iMac G3 took up less space.

Q11.
Give a score of 0, 1, or 2 based on how well the answer meets the criteria listed below.
- It should describe how Steve Jobs created a product that people would like when he made the iMac G3.
- It should use relevant details from the passage and the caption to show that the product was liked.

Q12. Use the 4-point rubric at the end of the answer key to give an overall score of 0, 1, 2, 3, or 4.

Practice Set 15

Question	Answer	Next Generation Learning Standard
1	C	Determine the meaning of words, phrases, figurative language, and academic and content-specific words.
2	C	Determine the meaning of words, phrases, figurative language, and academic and content-specific words.
3	A	In informational texts, identify and use text features to build comprehension.
4	B	In informational texts, describe the relationship among a series of events, ideas, concepts, or steps in a text, using language that pertains to time, sequence, and cause/effect.
5	B	Recognize genres and make connections to other texts, ideas, cultural perspectives, eras, personal events, and situations.
6	D	Determine a theme or central idea and explain how it is supported by key details; summarize portions of a text.
7	See Below	In informational texts, identify and use text features to build comprehension.
8	A	Determine the meaning of words, phrases, figurative language, and academic and content-specific words.
9	See Below	Explain how claims in a text are supported by relevant reasons and evidence.
10	See Below	In informational texts, describe the relationship among a series of events, ideas, concepts, or steps in a text, using language that pertains to time, sequence, and cause/effect.
11	See Below	Discuss how the reader's point of view or perspective may differ from that of the author, narrator or characters in a text.
12	See Below	Write an argument to support claim(s), using clear reasons and relevant evidence.

Q7.
Give a score of 0.5 for each section correctly listed. The possible sections are listed below.
- news, sport, home, travel, food, art, fashion, movies, or puzzles

Q9.
Give a score of 0, 1, or 2 based on how well the answer meets the criteria listed below.
- It should provide a reasonable explanation of the importance of the second sentence.
- The answer should show an understanding that the detail explains what a Pulitzer Prize is, shows the meaning of winning a Pulitzer Prize, or shows that *The New York Times* is known for excellent reporting.

Q10.
Give a score of 0, 1, or 2 based on how many correct differences are given.
- Possible answers include that it now costs more, that it sells fewer copies than it once did, or that it has to compete with online sites that offer news for free.

Q11.
Give a score of 0, 1, or 2 based on how well the answer meets the criteria listed below.
- It should state which details the student found most interesting.
- It should provide a fully-supported explanation of why the student found those details interesting.

Q12. Use the 4-point rubric at the end of the answer key to give an overall score of 0, 1, 2, 3, or 4.

Practice Set 16

Question	Answer	Next Generation Learning Standard
1	B	Determine the meaning of words, phrases, figurative language, and academic and content-specific words.
2	C	Develop and answer questions to locate relevant and specific details in a text to support an answer or inference.
3	2	In literary texts, identify parts of stories, dramas, and poems using terms such as chapter, scene, and stanza.
4	A	Determine the meaning of words, phrases, figurative language, and academic and content-specific words.
5	C	In literary texts, identify parts of stories, dramas, and poems using terms such as chapter, scene, and stanza.
6	C	Determine a theme or central idea and explain how it is supported by key details; summarize portions of a text.
7	A	Determine a theme or central idea and explain how it is supported by key details; summarize portions of a text.
8	little mighty	In literary texts, identify parts of stories, dramas, and poems using terms such as chapter, scene, and stanza.
9	See Below	Determine a theme or central idea and explain how it is supported by key details; summarize portions of a text.
10	See Below	Explain how specific illustrations or text features contribute to what is conveyed by the words in a text.
11	See Below	Develop and answer questions to locate relevant and specific details in a text to support an answer or inference.
12	See Below	Write narratives to develop real or imagined experiences or events using effective technique, descriptive details, and clear event sequences.

Q9.
Give a score of 0, 1, or 2 based on how well the answer meets the criteria listed below.
- It should explain that water, sand, and minutes all make up something much larger than themselves.

Q10.
Give a score of 0, 1, or 2 based on how well the answer meets the criteria listed below.
- It should identify the main idea as being about how little things can lead to greater things over time.
- It should show an understanding that the canyon is an example of something forming slowly over time.

Q11.
Give a score of 0, 1, or 2 based on how many relevant details from the caption are given.
- Possible answers include that the canyon took millions of years to form, that water wore the rock away a little at a time, or that the canyon is now thousands of feet deep.

Q12.
Give a score of 0, 1, 2, 3, or 4 based on how well the answer meets the criteria listed below.
- It should give a reasonable example of how the student's small actions led to something greater.
- It should show an understanding of the idea that small things can lead to greater things.

Practice Set 17

Question	Answer	Next Generation Learning Standard
1	B	Determine the meaning of words, phrases, figurative language, and academic and content-specific words.
2	B	Determine the meaning of words, phrases, figurative language, and academic and content-specific words.
3	B	Recognize genres and make connections to other texts, ideas, cultural perspectives, eras, personal events, and situations.
4	A	Explain how claims in a text are supported by relevant reasons and evidence.
5	C	Determine the meaning of words, phrases, figurative language, and academic and content-specific words.
6	A	Determine a theme or central idea and explain how it is supported by key details; summarize portions of a text.
7	See Below	In informational texts, identify and use text features to build comprehension.
8	See Below	Explain how specific illustrations or text features contribute to what is conveyed by the words in a text.
9	D	Explain how claims in a text are supported by relevant reasons and evidence.
10	B	Develop and answer questions to locate relevant and specific details in a text to support an answer or inference.
11	See Below	Determine a theme or central idea and explain how it is supported by key details; summarize portions of a text.
12	See Below	Write informative/explanatory texts to explore a topic and convey ideas and information relevant to the subject.

Q7.
Give a score of 0, 1, or 2 based on how many correct areas are given.
- The areas covered may include keeping fit and healthy, keeping active, reading and speaking, learning math, or learning English skills.

Q8.
Give a score of 0, 1, or 2 based on how well the answer meets the criteria listed below.
- It should identify the main purpose as being to describe some of the activities, to give examples of what the child will do, or to make the activities sound fun and/or useful.
- It should use relevant details from the passage.

Q11.
Give a score of 0, 1, or 2 based on how many acceptable reasons are given.
- Possible reasons listed could include that children under the age of five learn fitness habits they will keep for life, learn quickly, take in information quickly, and develop skills easier.

Q12. Use the 4-point rubric at the end of the answer key to give an overall score of 0, 1, 2, 3, or 4.

Practice Set 18

Question	Answer	Next Generation Learning Standard
1	B	In literary texts, describe character traits, motivations, or feelings, drawing on specific details from the text.
2	A	Develop and answer questions to locate relevant and specific details in a text to support an answer or inference.
3	D	In literary texts, identify parts of stories, dramas, and poems using terms such as chapter, scene, and stanza.
4	D	Explain how specific illustrations or text features contribute to what is conveyed by the words in a text.
5	See Below	Develop and answer questions to locate relevant and specific details in a text to support an answer or inference.
6	See Below	Discuss how the reader's point of view or perspective may differ from that of the author, narrator or characters in a text.
7	B	In literary texts, describe character traits, motivations, or feelings, drawing on specific details from the text.
8	B	Develop and answer questions to locate relevant and specific details in a text to support an answer or inference.
9	A	Determine a theme or central idea and explain how it is supported by key details; summarize portions of a text.
10	C	Explain how specific illustrations or text features contribute to what is conveyed by the words in a text.
11	See Below	Develop and answer questions to locate relevant and specific details in a text to support an answer or inference.
12	See Below	Recognize genres and make connections to other texts, ideas, cultural perspectives, eras, personal events, and situations.

Q5.
Give a score of 0, 1, or 2 based on how well the answer meets the criteria listed below.
- It should explain that Max is staying home, whereas Quinn and Hoy are going away.

Q6.
Give a score of 0, 1, or 2 based on how well the answer meets the criteria listed below.
- It should give a personal opinion on whether the plans sound interesting or dull. Either opinion is acceptable as long as it is supported.
- It should explain why the student has that opinion.

Q11.
Give a score of 0, 1, or 2 based on how well the answer meets the criteria listed below.
- The table should be completed with reasonable inferences about the setting and relevant details to support the inference. Sample answers are listed below.
- Where the story takes place / at a lake / They find a good spot near the lake.
- What time of day the story takes place / around noon / It is warm and gets warmer.
- What time of year the story takes place / summer / It is a warm day.

Q12. Use the 4-point rubric at the end of the answer key to give an overall score of 0, 1, 2, 3, or 4.

EXTENDED-RESPONSE SCORING RUBRIC

The extended-response questions are given a total score out of 4 based on the consideration of four factors. These factors and what to expect in a full-scoring answer are given below. Give students a score out of 4 based on how well the answer meets the criteria below overall.

Content and Analysis

The extent to which the essay conveys ideas and information clearly and accurately in order to support an analysis of topics or text.

A 4-point response will:
- clearly introduce a topic in a manner that follows logically from the task and purpose
- demonstrate comprehension and analysis of the text

Command of Evidence

The extent to which the essay presents evidence from the provided text to support analysis and reflection.

A 4-point response will:
- develop the topic with relevant, well-chosen facts, definitions, and details throughout the essay

Coherence, Organization, and Style

The extent to which the essay logically organizes complex ideas, concepts, and information using formal style and precise language.

A 4-point response will:
- clearly and consistently group related information together
- skillfully connect ideas within categories of information using linking words and phrases
- provide a concluding statement that follows clearly from the topic and information presented

Control of Conventions

The extent to which the essay demonstrates command of the conventions of standard English grammar, usage, capitalization, punctuation, and spelling.

A 4-point response will:
- demonstrate grade-appropriate command of conventions, with few errors

Get to Know Our Product Range

Mathematics

Practice Workbooks

Practice sets and practice tests will prepare students for the state tests.

Common Core Quiz Books

Focused individual quizzes cover every math skill one by one.

  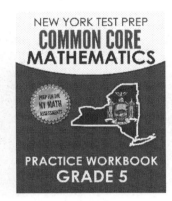

Reading

Practice Workbooks

Practice sets and practice tests will prepare students for the state tests.

Reading Skills Workbooks

Short passages and question sets will develop and improve reading comprehension skills and are perfect for ongoing test prep.

  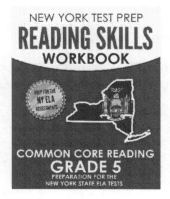

Writing

Writing Skills Workbooks
Students write narratives, essays, and arguments, and write in response to passages.

Narrative and Argument Writing Workbooks
Guided workbooks teach all the skills needed to write narratives and arguments.

  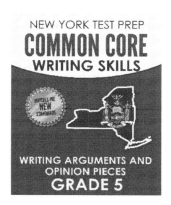

Language and Vocabulary

Language and Vocabulary Quiz Books
Focused quizzes cover spelling, grammar, usage, writing conventions, and vocabulary.

Revising and Editing Workbooks
Students improve language skills and writing skills by identifying and correcting errors.

Language Skills Workbooks
Exercises on specific language skills including figurative language, synonyms, and homographs.

http://www.testmasterpress.com